CUT
THE
CARBS!

CUT THE CARBS!

TORI HASCHKA

Photography by
CHRIS CHEN

Quadrille
PUBLISHING

FOR ANDREW AND WILL,
AKA THE HUNGRY ONES,
BIG AND SMALL.

CONTENTS

INTRODUCTION
6

UPLIFTING & FORTIFYING BREAKFASTS
12

LIGHT SNACKS TO SERVE WITH DRINKS
32

SOUPS (A DIFFERENT KIND
OF LIQUID LUNCH)
46

INTERESTING SIDES & SALADS
(FILLING ENOUGH TO FEED A 6'3" MAN)
64

LEAN SUMMER FEASTS
88

HUDDLE-BY-THE-FIRE COMFORT FOOD
118

MOREISH PUDDINGS
146

INDEX
172

INTRODUCTION

I know what it's like to use carbs as a culinary crutch. Until I was a teenager I would only eat things that were white. Rice, bread, potatoes, but most of all noodles. A little lick of butter, cheese or plain chicken was all the flavour I needed.

It wasn't until I was 21 and scoffing white rice and a small slick of curry in Malacca, Malaysia, that the tables really turned. The water I was sipping came from the local well. The meal was accompanied by a side order of E. coli. Soon after that, I got glandular fever. Then came five years of a spluttering immune system and exhaustion which felt like weights were attached to my legs and my brain was swaddled by marshmallow.

Suddenly, the foods I had turned to for comfort provided anything but. Not only did they not give me lasting energy, but they encouraged a sugar spike in my body which made me feel even worse.

And so I was lost. I had been conditioned to use white carbohydrates as the base of every meal I cooked. I assumed that because they sat at the bottom of the food pyramid I grew up with, that they were best for me. So Monday nights were quick stir-fries (with rice). Sometimes there were curries (with naan). The rest of the week: pizza, pasta, risotto, sushi. There was take-away Thai with my beloved Pad See Ew. Toasted sandwiches, plucked off the panini press. Baked potatoes with mince. Gnocchi with pesto. Sourdough toast with avocado and lemon juice for emergency late-night snacks. These were all quick, safe and relatively cheap. Those white carbohydrates were the blank canvas on top of which I pottered with other flavours.

As it turns out, the white carbohydrates that I had grown to love were foods which are broken down quickly in our bodies, swiftly transforming into glucose. Some of them left me feeling bloated. Some drove me to rabid hunger only a few hours after I'd eaten. And most would deliver a sharp jolt of energy, before leaving me more lethargic than I was to begin with.

The only way out I could find was to get creative in the kitchen. I needed to find some food that was smarter. And I needed to be a little cannier about how I cooked.

SO WHAT'S THE ANSWER?

I knew from the beginning that a strict no-carb doctrine was not for me. I'm not interested in brutal regimes; I love food too much. I take too much pleasure from gathering people around a table brimming with wine and conversation for an absolutist approach. I needed a moderate, middle path. But I was also starting to acknowledge the slightly uncomfortable truth A. A. Gill once expounded, that 'the easiest way to lose weight fast is to cut out carbs. Not all of them, but the big four: bread, potatoes, pasta, rice'.

I had to stop relying on the big four as my everyday, every-meal foods. Because losing a little bit of weight wasn't the only thing I could do with. The honest truth is that white carbohydrates were doing me no favours in lots of areas of my health. And the reason for that has to do with their glycaemic index.

What is the glycaemic index (GI)?

It's a way of ranking carbohydrates on a scale of 0–100 based on the impact they have on your blood sugar after you eat them. Foods scored with a high GI are digested swiftly and spike your blood sugar. Foods with a low GI are absorbed and digested more slowly, which has a more moderate, sustained effect on blood sugar, helping to keep you fuller for longer.

And which foods have some of the highest GIs of all? The big four: white bread, white rice, potatoes and white pasta.

What are smart carbs?

Carbohydrates help give us fuel. They have a significant role to play in our diets; even the most famous 'no-carb' doctrines incorporate carbohydrates again at some point. But a 'smart' carbohydrate is one which will work harder for you. Rather than eating a downy cloud of simple sugars, smart carbohydrates come packed with fibre, essential nutrients and amino acids.

What is the choice?

The choice between filling up on smart carbs or simple white ones is akin to packing a suitcase for a trip. On one hand, you've got the option of taking with you a variety of clothes, three pairs of shoes and your toiletries. On the other you could just cram a white fluffy duvet into your bag. Sure the duvet will cover you for a brief period, but its usefulness will soon wear out.

NEW FOODS, NEW OPTIONS, NEW LIFE

I know better than anyone that the comfort of white carbs can be difficult to leave behind. For one, we associate them with filling us up, at least in the short term. For me, one of the hardest things was finding new meals that would also satisfy my 6'3" husband. I've referred to him for years as 'The Hungry One'. And while it's a name that applies to his appetite for life as much as his ability to consume, most who know him will agree: the man can eat. Straight soups and salads with grilled protein just weren't going to cut it.

Slow-burning carbohydrates that could provide proper substance needed to take centre stage. That was one way to prevent him churning through dinner and then at the end gently asking what was for main course.

Since then, I've fallen for protein-rich grains and seeds like quinoa, chia, ground flaxseed/linseed. I've become a little evangelical about pulses, replacing the staple side of mashed potatoes and rice with white bean purée, and convinced others that not only is it quicker, but often tastier too. I found that chickpea flour has a nutty flavour that works particularly well in savoury dishes. And when it comes to sweets, instead of my default desserts of bread pudding, tarts and pies, I learned to love baking with ground nuts and use fruits as a base.

Once I started cooking this way, I quickly learned that a change really can be as good as a holiday. And I'm not alone. Friends and colleagues with diabetes, heart conditions and polycystic ovaries, those who are breastfeeding and those who just want to lose a little bit of excess weight, have all benefitted from shifting away from white carbs – and they've never looked back.

Concentrating on eating smart carbs when we're at home has made a world of difference to my life. I'm healthier. I have more energy. My skin is better. I lost four kilos from what I thought was my standard weight (and The Hungry One has lost six). When I got pregnant with baby Will, I found it tempting to fall down a deep and dark carb hole. And I certainly had my moments: the first thing I ate after he was born was a toasted ham, cheese and tomato sandwich, and nothing has ever tasted better. But eating slower and smarter carbs as the base of most meals not only allowed me to shed most of the pregnancy weight, but gave me the right sort of energy in the first three months of his life to balance feeding him, taking care of him, and writing and testing the recipes for this book.

These recipes take inspiration from both my travels and my life in Sydney and London. They fill us up and pack a flavour punch. They're celebratory, but in a low-key sort of way. This food is fresh, vibrant and addictively good. What you'll find is not really a diet at all; It's just a new way of looking at what you eat. There are some new ingredients to fall in love with and some makeovers for old friends.

Hopefully you'll find that some small shifts can make a big difference. But the biggest change for me since we started eating this way has been that on the days when I go to enjoy pasta, bread, rice or potatoes, I do it because I really want to savour every bite, not just because I can't think of anything else that's good to eat.

SOME NEW (AND OLD) FRIENDS FOR A SMART-CARB KITCHEN

Quinoa and quinoa flakes

While it might look like a grain, quinoa (pronounced 'keen-wa') is actually a South American seed from the goosefoot plant. It's high in protein and contains essential vitamins and minerals such as calcium, phosphorus and iron. It comes in a variety of colours, has a nutty flavour and benefits from being rinsed before cooking. The flakes can be used as a porridge, or in baking, and the seeds make a sturdy side for dishes like Peach Pulled Pork with Dirty Quinoa, and Prawn and Quinoa Grits.

Chia seeds

Closely resembling poppy seeds, chia seeds are packed with essential fatty acids like Omega-3, fibre, protein and minerals like calcium, zinc and iron. When combined with liquid, they swell up into small orbs. Most of the benefit is found when they're eaten raw, like in the Chia, Mango, Coconut and Macadamia Trifle, Chia Bircher Muesli, or sprinkled on top of salads, but they're also a good source of fibre when cooked in the Peppers Stuffed with Chia, Hummus and Pine Nuts, for example.

Linseed/flaxseed

The seeds from the flax plant have a light caramel and oatey flavour and are an excellent way to reduce the amount of white flour used in baking recipes. They are a great source of Omega-3, fibre and antioxidants.

Chickpea (besan or gram) flour

Chickpea flour (also known as besan or gram flour) is made from ground chickpeas or chana dal. It's a common ingredient in Indian and Bangladeshi cooking and you can usually find it cheaply in Indian grocery stores. It's a great substitute for white flour in savoury dishes, whether for dusting fishcakes, or making béchamel. It's also a key ingredient in socca, the chickpea pancakes common to Nice.

Rice malt syrup

Rice malt syrup is a sweetener made of complex carbohydrates. You can use it in place of honey or syrups in many recipes, like the glaze for the Pigs in Kimchee Blankets on page 39, or try it as a substitute for sugar to balance the flavours in many of the savoury recipes, too.

Apple cider vinegar

Beyond its terrific balance of sweetness and acidity which helps to brighten recipes as diverse as dal to dressings for Brussels sprouts and lentils, the acetic acid in apple cider vinegar is reputed to help prevent the build-up of fat in our bodies.

A FEW NOTES ABOUT PULSES

Pulses are some of the real heroes in this book. Eating more lentils, beans and chickpeas is a key way to stay full for longer. They're excellent sources of fibre. Yet there are a couple of key reasons why people don't eat as much of them as they should.

The soaking factor

True, you will get the best results from most of these recipes if you use dried pulses, soak them and then cook them from scratch. The texture will probably be superior and you'll find the GI of your pulses can be even lower if they avoid the canning process. But how many of us will remember to put a key ingredient for tomorrow's dinner on to soak before we go to bed, or while we eat breakfast? The answer lies in tinned pulses. Stock your cupboard with cannellini beans, borlotti beans, black beans, adzuki beans, lentils and chickpeas. They're cheap and last for an age. Organic ones will have a better texture. Just be sure to rinse them well of all of the liquid before using them. (You may also want to look for tins which are BPA-free.)

If you prefer to use dried pulses, in any recipe that specifies 1 x 400-g tin of beans, rinsed, feel free to substitute 90–100 g dried beans or pulses, then soak and cook them according to the timings opposite.

Soaking and cooking times

BEAN SIZE	SOAKING TIME	COOKING METHOD
Large beans: kidney, chickpea, borlotti, cannellini	6–8 hours	Drain soaking liquid and cover with water, plus 3 cm. Bring to the boil, then simmer for 1–2 hours. Simmer uncovered for firmer beans, or covered for creamier, softer beans. Drain, if necessary, then serve.
Medium beans: black beans, pinto	4–6 hours	Drain soaking liquid and cover with water, plus 3 cm. Bring to the boil, then simmer for 40–60 minutes. Simmer uncovered for firmer beans, or covered for creamier, softer beans. Drain, if necessary, then serve.
Small beans: mung, adzuki	4 hours	Drain soaking liquid and cover with water, plus 3–5 cm. Bring to the boil, then simmer for 30 minutes. Simmer uncovered for firmer beans, or covered for creamier, softer beans. Drain, if necessary, then serve.
Split peas, chana dal, lentils	Not strictly necessary, though 1 hour will benefit	Drain soaking liquid and cover with water, plus 3–5 cm. Bring to the boil, then simmer for 30–45 minutes. Simmer uncovered for firmer beans, or covered for creamier, softer beans. Drain, if necessary, then serve.

The gas factor

Nobody likes to talk about it. But I guess if you had to pinpoint one reason why people don't eat as many pulses as perhaps they should, they'll mention the gas factor. In addition to the fact that the more you eat of them, the more your body gets used to digesting them, there are certain things you can do to help mitigate this side effect. The first is to dispose of both the soaking and cooking water and to rinse your pulses well. The second involves adding certain things to them while you cook them.

There are amino acids in seaweed, kombu and kelp which help make the beans more digestible. Try adding some in when you cook them next time, or try the Ultimate Ham and Lentil Soup which makes use of nori for exactly this purpose.

Spices and flavourings like cumin, turmeric, ginger, coriander and lemon are all reputed to help ameliorate some of the gassy effects. Many of the recipes in this book, from the Mexican Baked Eggs, Smokey Baked Beans, Chilled Chickpea Soup, Dal, Yellow Split Peas with Ginger, and Tandoori Salmon with Spiced Lentils all use these to help.

Start as you mean to go on. A day that begins with a sustaining breakfast has a better chance of being a good one (or at least a slimmer chance of encouraging you to get intimate with a tin of chocolate biscuits at 10.42am). Most mornings for me begin with either a cinnamon coffee protein shake, a small smoked paprika chia frittata (if I've made a batch earlier in the week) or bircher muesli or porridge made from chia or quinoa.

By the time the weekends roll around we've now clocked that breakfast and brunch are a great occasion to entertain, particularly if there are wee ones involved. That's when a generous portion of Smokey Baked Beans or a tray of Mexican Baked Eggs come to the fore. They're a relatively easy, prepare-ahead way to put food on the table for a group – with the added benefit of nobody needing to be on toast duty. The only thing left to organise is who's making the coffee.

UPLIFTING
& FORTIFYING
BREAKFASTS

CINNAMON COFFEE PROTEIN SHAKES

Serves 1

There are days when you need breakfast to be in liquid form; when haste is high and the morning calls for something you can quickly consume (often with one hand, while running a comb through your hair and feeding a small person with the other). These cinnamon coffee protein shakes are my solution. The coffee gives a bit of get-up-and-go, the flaxseed/ linseed adds fibre and the cinnamon is festive. Be sure to shake or blend it well to prevent any gritty clumps. And if you're after a little extra ballast, a banana or some silken tofu blended through works a treat.

375 ml milk (almond, milk, soy, cow or whatever
   takes your fancy)
1–2 scoops of your preferred protein powder
   (coffee, chocolate or neutrally flavoured is best)
2 tbsp ground flaxseed/linseed
1 shot of espresso or 30 ml strong coffee
1 tsp ground cinnamon
2 ice cubes

Optional extras
1 banana; 1 tbsp raw cacao (if using a neutral-tasting protein
   powder); 100 g silken tofu

Equipment
a blender that can crush ice cubes

Put all the ingredients in a blender and blitz until smooth. Pour it into a glass.

If you prefer a little more body, add the banana and blend again until smooth. If you want an extra whack of protein, add the silken tofu. I bet on the tasting you'll never know it was there.

ALMOND BLUEBERRY PANCAKES

Makes 10–12 pancakes, or serves 2–3

The best blueberry pancakes in the world arguably hail from the Clinton Street Baking Company in New York's East Village. These are not those pancakes. But these pancakes also don't require you to jog up to Central Park and pound out a few laps of The Reservoir before you're ready to face lunch. The body and bulk of white flour is here replaced with ground flaxseed/linseed and ground almonds but you'll still find the adorable puff from egg whites and pop from blistered berries. Add some yoghurt and flaked almonds on the side and you're good to go.

250 ml milk
120 g ground flaxseed/linseed
50 g ground almonds
2 tbsp vegetable oil
4 eggs, separated
a pinch of salt
1 tbsp butter
125 g blueberries

To serve
ground cinnamon, yoghurt and flaked toasted almonds;
   additional blueberries or sliced banana (optional)

Mix together the milk, flaxseed/linseed, almonds, vegetable oil and egg yolks in a bowl.

In a separate bowl, add the salt and egg whites and whisk until you get soft peaks. Fold them into the batter in 2 stages, trying to keep as much air in as possible.

Heat a non-stick frying or pancake pan over medium– high heat and swipe with the butter. Dollop in 3 tablespoons of the batter and scatter a tablespoon of the blueberries over the top. Cook for 3–4 minutes until you can lift the bottom of the pancake and it is brown. Use a large spatula or fish slice to gently flip the pancake over, then cook the other side for about 1–2 minutes. Keep it warm in a low oven while you make the remaining pancakes.

Serve the pancakes with the cinnamon, yoghurt, flaked almonds, more blueberries or slices of banana, if you like.

MUSHROOM AND GOATS' CURD 'TOASTIES'

Serves 2

A toastie for breakfast has rescued many a morning, and one of the things I missed the most when I converted to a slow/low carb start to the day. Here, a perennial favourite – mushroom, goats' cheese, spinach and basil – is reborn by replacing the bread with flat Portobello mushrooms, protecting a melting interior of cheese and greens. There's a little avocado on top (because to an Australian, it's hard to have a proper breakfast without some avocado on the plate) and some pine nuts for crunch. Add a wedge of lemon for a little sunshine and it's happy-making fodder.

Take this concept and adapt it to your heart's content. Swap around the fillings: try mozzarella for extra molten pull, or a slice of ham. And if you feel like breakfast isn't breakfast without eggs, feel free to scramble a couple to join in the fun on the side.

4 large, flat Portobello mushrooms, stems removed (you can remove the stems by wiggling them from side to side, then twisting them up and out; save them for stock or salads)
1 tbsp olive oil, plus extra to drizzle
2 handfuls of baby spinach or cavolo nero
2 tbsp goats' curd
½ avocado, deseeded and cut into slim slices
12 fresh basil leaves
2 tbsp pine nuts, toasted
sea salt and freshly ground black pepper
wedges of lemon, to serve

Equipment
panini press

Turn on the panini press and brush the top and bottom of the mushrooms with the olive oil.

Layer the spinach in the dark brown bellies of 2 of the mushrooms and dab the goats' curd around on top. Sandwich with the other 2 mushrooms so the dark brown bellies are facing inwards. Place the sandwiches in the preheated panini press. If you are having difficulty getting the press to close, use metal tongs to grip the outside of the mushrooms to help chock the press at the right height. Toast the sandwiches for 5 minutes or until the mushrooms are cooked through. Transfer the sandwiches to a sheet of kitchen paper and allow the juices to seep out for a minute.

Put some avocado slices, basil leaves and pine nuts on top of the toasties, season with salt and pepper and serve with lemon wedges.

GOOEY EGGS WITH ASPARAGUS DIPPERS

Serves 1, though easily doubles, triples etc

Oh... The Wolseley. This bastion of civility in the heart of London is an institution for a reason. Some people, when entering, may crave the viennoiserie, with the croissants baked fresh every morning by the in-house tourier, but for me it's hard to go past the soft eggs with soldiers, served in a novelty double-headed cup. A perfectly cooked and coddled egg is the epitome of nursery comfort. Yet when you're not eating breakfast in such perfectly adult surroundings, you might crave something more refined than fingers of toast for dunking in your gooey yolk. To me there is no finer implement than a spear of steamed asparagus. Season it and the egg well with a little salt and black pepper. If you want a bit more protein, encircle your trimmed green stems in prosciutto. When I want a touch of elegance in my morning and I can't make it to the hushed marble dining rooms at 160 Piccadilly, this is exactly what I turn to. Now if only I could get hold of a double-headed cup.

2 eggs at room temperature
8 asparagus spears, trimmed
8 strips of prosciutto or jamón, or thin-cut leg ham (optional)
olive oil
sea salt and freshly ground black pepper

Bring a saucepan of water to a rolling boil. Submerge the eggs and boil for 5 minutes and 15 seconds.

While the eggs are cooking, steam the asparagus in a steamer basket above the eggs until they are soft – around 3 minutes.

For a little bit of extra flavour, wrap each asparagus spear in the prosciutto or jamón. Drizzle with olive oil and season with a little salt and pepper.

Carefully cut the top off each egg and dip the asparagus spears into the yolk before eating the remaining white with a small spoon.

SMOKED PAPRIKA CHIA FRITTATAS

Makes 8 mini frittatas, or serves 2–3

Breakfast in Barcelona: the gentle sog of pan con tomate – ripe tomatoes ground into griddled white bread, drizzled with olive oil and seasoned with salt and occasionally a sprinkle of smoked paprika. Add a curl of cured pork and a cortado coffee and a great day is made. Here we take the same flavours and turn them into something a little more sustaining for life back at home. These mini-frittatas are a fistful of protein; from the eggs, to the surprising bulk of plumped chia seeds to the collar of crisp bacon (or jamón). Make them in a non-stick muffin tin and serve them with some rocket and lemon for a swift breakfast. Or stuff a couple in a Tupperware and tote it to work while you dream about the next chance you'll have to get away.

8 strips of streaky bacon or jamón, cut in half crossways
200 g cherry tomatoes
1 garlic clove
1 tbsp smoked paprika
85 g chia seeds
4 eggs, lightly beaten
1 tsp sea salt

To serve
rocket and lemon wedges

Equipment
1 x 12-hole non-stick muffin tin, greased (if your tin is not non-stick, line the base of each hole with a round of baking paper)

Preheat the oven to 180°C/350°F/Gas 4.

Line the inside of 8 muffin-tin holes with 2 half-strips of bacon, overlapping them to ensure that the whole perimeter is covered.

Use a stick blender or food processor to blend together the cherry tomatoes, garlic and paprika until smooth. Stir together with the chia seeds, eggs and salt.

Pour the batter into the bacon-lined muffin-tin holes.

Bake the frittatas in the preheated oven for 30 minutes or until the bacon is brown, the frittatas are puffed and the tops are firm to the touch.

Serve with rocket and a wedge of lemon to squeeze over the frittatas.

FETA, MINT, LENTIL AND PISTACHIO OMELETTES

Serves 2

Lentils and eggs are the suggested power-breakfast of many slow-carb regimes. Here's a way to turn what can be a motley mess on a plate – the sort of thing that a college boy will shovel in his mouth before hitting a weights room that smells of Tuesday's socks – into a meal you can be proud of.

5 tbsp olive oil
1 x 400-g tin of brown lentils, rinsed and drained
2 large handfuls of baby spinach
1 tsp sea salt
50 g Persian (marinated) feta, crumbled
6 eggs
4 tbsp fresh mint leaves, roughly torn
2 tbsp pistachios, toasted
freshly ground black pepper

To serve
lemon wedges and chilli sauce

Place 1 tablespoon of the olive oil in a non-stick frying pan and add the lentils, spinach and salt. Stir to warm the ingredients through and wilt the spinach. Season with pepper and transfer the contents of the pan to a plate. Crumble the Persian feta over the top of the lentils and set aside while you make your omelettes.

Whisk the eggs together in a bowl. Heat 2 tablespoons of the olive oil in the frying pan and add half of the egg mixture, swirling the pan to coat the base. Cook for 2 minutes or until the top of the omelette is almost set and base is golden.

Spoon half of the lentil mixture over the half of the omelette that's furthest away from you. Use firm shakes of the pan to jerk the nearest edge of the omelette up the lip of the pan. Use a spatula to fold the nearest half over the filling to enclose it. Slide the omelette onto a plate and scatter with half of the mint leaves and pistachios. Serve with a wedge of lemon and some chilli sauce. Repeat with the remaining oil, eggs and lentil mixture to make a second omelette and garnish with the remaining mint and pistachios.

CHIA BIRCHER MUESLI

Makes 2–4 breakfast portions depending on
what you want to have it with and how hungry
you are first thing in the morning

My previous experience with chia was via an allergy-safe pet, shorn with child-friendly scissors. These days it's a new 'wonderfood'. It's supposedly got more omega-3 than salmon and it's packed full of protein. I've found when dry that it can get stuck in your molars in a way that you thought only a strawberry seed could. But saturate the seeds in a little liquid and they swell up like cheerful orbs of freckled tapioca.

There are very few things that make me happier in the morning than knowing that breakfast is ready-cued in the fridge – which is how this muesli substitute was born. To these friendly seeds I add ground flaxseed/linseed, yoghurt, milk and a few stray berries for a little fruitiness and flavour. They all hang out together in the fridge overnight and meld into a silky, bircher-esque mass. What you then have is a quick but slow (carb) breakfast option that doesn't involve lentils, bacon or eggs.

I'll sometimes top a portion with a few extra toasted nuts, berries or seeds – and for the full, more traditional bircher experience, I'll add in a grated apple, skin and all. But most often it's just eaten as is, swiftly out of a bowl, while I wait for the kettle to boil and a good day to roll.

85 g chia seeds
50 g rolled oats
375 g plain yoghurt (sheep, goat, soy or whatever takes
  your fancy)
45 g ground flaxseed/linseed (though feel free to substitute
  with bran or oats if you want some more slow-release carbs)
2 handfuls of berries, smooshed with a fork (fresh or frozen)
315 ml milk

Optional extras
Grated apple, or bran or ground almonds (in which case,
  add the same quantity of yoghurt or milk, so it doesn't
  all become too dry); a handful of diced dried pear and
  some chopped Brazil nuts or almonds; fresh berries
  or ½ passionfruit

Equipment
Large tupperware of at least 1-litre capacity

Mix the chia seeds, oats and yoghurt together well to
incorporate.

Add the flaxseed/linseed, smooshed berries and milk.
Stir very well to prevent globby masses of chia forming
in the corners.

Place in the fridge for at least 2 hours to soak and
incorporate, or overnight.

Stir well once more before serving. Eat on its own,
or with some additional fruit, yoghurt and seeds for
extra flavour and crunch.

CHAI AND APRICOT QUINOA PORRIDGE

Serves 2

A cup of tea and a bowl of porridge – this is how most good mornings should commence. Yet there's no reason why they shouldn't be melded together. And porridge need not just be the domain of oats. Quinoa flakes are a novel addition to your pantry (and often stocked in supermarkets, or your local healthfood store). They swell and plump up just like the warming cereals your Nan used to make you on frosty mornings. They're also ripe for adopting other flavours while they cook. This version uses the warmth of chai tea bags with the zip of dried apricots and hazelnuts, though you could just as easily employ Earl Grey or Darjeeling with some dates or prunes. With a small amount of dried fruit or a swirl of jam, some yoghurt and some nuts for crunch, you'll be set for the day.

250 ml milk
250 ml boiling water
2 chai tea bags
100 g rolled quinoa flakes
3 tbsp chopped dried apricots or 2 tbsp apricot jam
3 tbsp chopped hazelnuts
2 tbsp plain yoghurt, to serve

Bring the milk and water to a simmer in a saucepan. Add the tea bags and allow to steep for 5 minutes.

Discard the tea bags, then add the quinoa flakes and half of the dried apricots to the liquid. Bring to the boil, then reduce to a simmer and place the lid on. Cook for 10 minutes or until the quinoa is soft and most of the liquid has been absorbed.

Remove from the heat and portion into bowls. Top with the remaining dried apricots (or apricot jam), hazelnuts and yoghurt.

TIP: *Other good combinations to try along with chai are a lick of fig and ginger jam with pistachios, blackcurrant jam with flaked almonds, or some mashed banana with diced Brazil nuts.*

SOFT EGGS WITH SMOKEY BAKED BEANS

Serves 4

Proper, satisfying baked beans cry out for the aroma of a fire. They should be crafted in battered metal pots over coals, combining pork, pulses and a vista that can make you swoon a little. If you can't make it to the great outdoors (or have an innate aversion to the possibility of having ants crawl up your legs while you cook), you can always ape the mystical aroma of fire with a few drops of liquid smoke (available from many gourmet food stores). Shhh, I won't tell if you don't.

For a life-affirming feast all you need are a few soft eggs, a cairn of beans and a strong cup of coffee to the side. The yolks will bleed like a sunrise and the caffeine will give you a proper kick along for whatever you've got planned – even if it's just an afternoon on the couch watching Brokeback Mountain one more time.

(If you are planning on making these while out on an intrepid adventure, you can always mix all of the spices, dry ingredients and sauces together into a slurry at home and tote it along in a glass jar.)

1 tbsp olive oil

125 g bacon, finely diced

2 pork or beef sausages, skin removed and contents rumpled

1 red onion, peeled and cut into slim half-moons

3 garlic cloves, thinly sliced or grated

2 x 400-g tins of chopped tomatoes

1 tbsp Worcestershire sauce

2 tbsp tomato paste

2 tbsp dark brown muscovado sugar

1 tbsp apple cider vinegar

1 tbsp Dijon mustard

1 x 400-g tin of borlotti beans, rinsed

1 x 400-g tin of butter or cannellini beans, rinsed

100 g cherry tomatoes

1 tsp sea salt

1 tsp liquid smoke (optional)

1 tbsp bicarbonate of soda

4 eggs at room temperature (older eggs are better)

2 tbsp fresh flat-leaf parsley leaves, roughly chopped

Put the olive oil, bacon and sausagemeat in a heavy-based saucepan or casserole dish over medium heat. Sauté for 3 minutes or until the bacon has started to gain some colour.

Add the onion and garlic and sauté for 5–7 minutes until they have begun to soften. Add the chopped tomatoes, Worcestershire sauce, tomato paste, sugar, vinegar and mustard and bring to a simmer, uncovered.

Add the beans and tomatoes and cook, stirring occasionally, for 15 minutes or until the sauce has reduced, is thick and is clinging to the beans. Taste and season with the salt to bring the flavours together, and the liquid smoke if you fancy a faux outdoorsy twist.

To cook the eggs, bring a saucepan of water to a rolling boil. Add the bicarbonate of soda and eggs to the boiling water. Boil the eggs for 5 minutes. Remove them from the pan and run them briefly under cold water. Gently tap the shells against a hard surface and peel them, being careful not to puncture the yolk. Place the peeled eggs in a bowl of warm water until ready to serve.

Serve the beans in bowls with the eggs nestled on top and sprinkled with the parsley. Allow the yolk to seep into the beans while eating.

TIP: *When boiling the eggs, adding the bicarbonate of soda to the water helps encourage the shells to shirk away from the whites, making them exponentially easier to peel.*

MEXICAN BAKED EGGS

Serves 4–6

Everyone needs a few self-sufficient breakfast recipes. The sort of thing that you can pull together when you're feeling a touch dusty, perhaps from the pleasures of a few too many margaritas the night prior. Baked eggs are a saviour. There's no need to faff about with poaching or scrambling to order – just crack a few eggs over a base of spiced black beans and plop them in the oven while you go about organising juices and caffeine. These ones have a south-of-the border accent. Serve them with a good thwack of guacamole and some hot sauce and you've got a breakfast that can pull anyone back from the brink, no matter how many shots of Patrón you sipped.

2 red peppers, halved and deseeded
250 g cherry tomatoes, halved
1 tbsp olive oil, plus extra if needed
50 g chorizo, diced (optional)
1 red onion, peeled and diced
1 small chilli, diced (and deseeded if you don't like things too hot)
1 tbsp ground cumin
½ tbsp ground coriander
1 pinch of dried chilli flakes
1 large handful of fresh coriander, stems finely chopped and leaves reserved
2 x 400-g tins of black beans, rinsed
10 g dark chocolate (minimum 70% cocoa solids)
1 tsp chipotle purée or ½ tsp ground chipotle (optional)
4 eggs
4 tsp Greek yoghurt
sea salt and freshly ground black pepper

Guacamole
2 ripe avocados, deseeded and peeled
squeeze of lemon or lime juice
chilli sauce (optional)

Equipment
4–6 ramekins or small ovenproof bowls

Preheat the oven to 150°C/300°F/Gas 2.

Drizzle the peppers and tomatoes with the olive oil and place in the preheated oven to roast for 45 minutes or until lightly blistered. (You can do this the night before if you prefer, or substitute with roasted peppers from a jar, in which case just throw the fresh tomatoes in when you add the beans.)

Place the diced chorizo in a heavy-based saucepan or casserole dish over medium heat. Sauté it until it starts to leach crimson oil. If it is a drier chorizo, you may want to add 1–2 tablespoons olive oil to the pan, then throw in the onion, fresh chilli, cumin, coriander, chilli flakes and coriander stems.

Sauté for 5–7 minutes or until the onion has softened. Add the black beans, chocolate and chipotle, if using, and stir to combine.

Take the roasted peppers out of the oven and leave them to cool just until you can handle them without burning yourself. Raise the oven temperature to 180°C/350°F/Gas 4.

Slice the peppers and add them, along with the roasted tomatoes and the oil they cooked in, to the pan with the beans. Stir to combine. Taste and adjust the seasoning with salt and pepper and more chilli if you want.

Place 2–3 tablespoons of the bean mixture in the bottom and up the sides of each ramekin, creating a well in the centre. Ensure there's at least 2 cm clear at the top for your egg. Place the ramekins on a baking tray.

Gently crack an egg into each ramekin, taking care not to puncture the yolk. Float a teaspoon of Greek yoghurt over the top of the yolk. You can leave your eggs like this until you're ready to eat.

When your guests have arrived and just before you're ready to eat, put the ramekins in the oven and bake them for 10–12 minutes or until the whites are solid but the yolks are still a little runny.

While they're baking, make a quick guacamole by mashing the avocado with the chopped coriander, a squeeze of citrus and a little chilli sauce, if you like. Serve the baked eggs with the guacamole.

TIP: *This will leave you with a little extra beans. They're delicious as a warm salad later on.*

SOCCA WITH SMOKED SALMON AND WHIPPED CURDS

Makes 10–12 pancakes depending
on the size of your pan, or serves 4

Introducing socca, the sturdy chickpea flour pancakes that are one of the favoured street foods of Nice. They're burnished and have the rough texture of burlap bags. Their taste is nutty and there's a satisfying mix of crisp edges and pliant pockets of batter. They're best served with a bit of rosemary, olive oil and salt while you sip pink wine and play a novel game of hypothesising which super-yacht you'd buy if you stumbled across a cool ten million pounds.

They're delightful at the cusp of a day, but they'd also make a lovely snack at the close with a pile of marinated olives and some goats' curd and chunks of fennel on the side.

350 g chickpea (besan or gram) flour, sifted
125 ml olive oil
800 ml lukewarm water
1 tsp ground cumin, to add a slightly smokey flavour
  (optional)
sea salt, to balance any bitterness in the chickpea flour
butter or olive oil, to grease
340 g cottage cheese
2 tsp apple cider vinegar
1 tsp honey or rice malt syrup
2 spring onions, diced
200 g smoked salmon

Equipment
a non-stick frying or pancake pan is vital

Combine the chickpea flour and olive oil, whisking them together with a balloon whisk. Whisk in the water and cumin, if using, and leave to rest for 30 minutes. Taste a little of the batter and add salt if it seems bitter.

Heat a non-stick frying or pancake pan over medium heat and swipe with butter or olive oil. Pour in just enough batter to coat the bottom and swirl around. Cook until you can easily lift the pancake from the bottom of the pan. Use a large spatula or fish slice to gently flip the pancake over, then cook the other side until browned. Keep it warm in a low oven while you make the remaining pancakes.

Blend the cottage cheese with the vinegar and honey until smooth.

To assemble, stack the pancakes with the cottage cheese and spring onions. Top with smoked salmon.

TIP: *Be sure to taste the batter before you start – if you're using unroasted chickpea flour it can have a bitter taste. This can be mitigated by adding more salt. Also be sure to whisk the batter well before starting, as the flour sediment can sink to the bottom of the bowl. The first pancake may be no good. This happens. Be sure that your pan is well greased before starting.*

TIP: *You can usually find chickpea flour (sometimes known as besan or gram) in the Indian section of a supermarket.*

BLACK FOREST SLOW GRANOLA PARFAITS

Serves 4–6

This granola takes the alchemic combination of cocoa, cherries and dairy and puts them to a more restrained use than in a slice of torte. There are a few secrets to golden granola; chief among them is using egg whites to help the grains gather into plump clumps. Beyond that there's olive oil for superior crunch, ensuring there's a good mix of grains and only adding the dried fruit after the grains have been baked. Be sure to add whatever nuts are your favourite – mine are macadamias and hazelnuts – but almonds and walnuts would also be grand. All that's left is to add a pinch or two of salt to curb the sweetness and keep this giddily delicious combination at the adult end of the spectrum. You may be eating cocoa for breakfast, but this layered treat is a long way from the domain of snap, crackle and pop.

80 g rolled oats
45 g ground flaxseed/linseed
30 g desiccated coconut
60 g hazelnuts, roughly chopped
30 g macadamia nuts, roughly chopped
2 tsp ground cinnamon
3 tbsp cocoa powder
1–2 tsp sea salt flakes
4 tbsp olive oil
60 ml rice malt syrup or pure maple syrup
1 egg white, beaten until foamy
150 g dried cherries

To serve
900 g Greek yoghurt and 200 g drained
  Morello cherries

Equipment
baking tray lined with baking paper

Preheat the oven to 140°C/285°F/Gas 1.

Mix all the dry ingredients together (except the dried cherries) in a big bowl.

Heat the olive oil and syrup together in a small pan until bubbling and pour the mixture over the dry ingredients in the bowl.

Mix everything together until well coated, then fold through the beaten egg white. Pour it onto the lined baking tray and bake in the preheated oven for 45 minutes. Turn the granola over with a spoon, return it to the oven and bake for another 25 minutes or until the nuts are crunchy. Allow it to cool for 15 minutes, then break up the clumps.

Combine the granola clumps with the dried cherries. Either put the granola in an airtight container to keep, or assemble the parfaits.

To assemble the parfaits, take 4 glasses or tumblers and layer them with yoghurt, cherries and granola, then more yoghurt, cherries and granola. Serve immediately.

Drinks and nibbles can be a slightly sticky time if you're trying to avoid the starches. The reason? Bread. It's the standard fodder we lean on to help fill a hole before a meal commences; whether grissini with olives, pita with dips or charred bruschetta. Yet as soon as you start thinking outside the box you'll discover a wide arena of alternative snacks and starters.

Whether it's a whole steamed artichoke which starts as a table decoration before being slowly dismantled petal by petal and dragged through aïoli, or the perfect recipe for kale crisps (which really became that popular for a reason), you'll be set.

As for us, if it's just a Friday night at home celebrating the close of a long week The Hungry One will usually open the canisters of five-spice soy almonds and spiced chickpea bombs which live in the pantry while he cracks through a beer. If we've got guests gathered around the barbecue then it's roasted tomato and halloumi skewers and some cannellini bean dip with crudités. And if I'm feeling cheeky and festive, then it's hard to walk away from a platter of pigs in kimchee blankets. As long as there's a mix of bright spice and crunch (and something cheerful in a glass to go with it), we're happy.

LIGHT SNACKS TO SERVE WITH DRINKS

CANNELLINI BEAN, PARMESAN AND ARTICHOKE DIP WITH CRUDITÉS

Makes 1.5 cups, or serves 4–6

I can usually be trusted to behave at a party. I'll bring something nice to eat, a chilled bottle of wine and a pair of shoes that says 'I care enough to not wear sneakers to your soirée, but I can still stand in these for an hour'. I can be perfectly social, except when this dip is on offer. Because then there's every chance I'm going to take a small bowl and run away to a quiet corner and scoff it all. There's something about the unsung, holy trinity of artichokes, Parmesan and pale pulses. It's a communion of earth and brightness, the Parmesan adds richness, the pulses offer a mild sweetness and the artichokes contribute a curious twang of acid. I've leaned on this trio before in a simple braise with chicken thighs, leeks, stock and baby spinach but I think it's here, in a dip made solid with white beans and served with crisp crudités, that their charms really come to the fore.

1 x 285-g jar of marinated artichoke hearts (170–200 g drained artichokes, but reserve the marinade)
1 x 400-g tin of cannellini beans, rinsed
1 tbsp fresh flat-leaf parsley leaves, roughly chopped
30 g Parmesan, grated
grated zest and juice of ½ lemon
½ tsp freshly ground black pepper

To serve
1 bunch of baby carrots, scrubbed clean; 1 fennel bulb, bottom trimmed, and cut into slim wedges; cherry tomatoes, on skewers

Spoon 2 tablespoons of the artichoke heart marinade into a blender. Drain the rest.

Add the artichoke hearts, cannellini beans, parsley, Parmesan, lemon zest and juice, and the black pepper. Blend until smooth. If it is too thick, add 1–2 tablespoons of hot water or olive oil to create a more pliable, dip-like consistency.

Serve the dip with the crudités.

RADISHES WITH BUTTER AND TRUFFLE SALT

Serves 4

Sometimes I like to pretend I'm in France – or that I'm much more soignée than I am. One way is to pull out a Breton striped shirt and a silk scarf. The other way is to serve this dish to guests. Radishes with butter and salt are a classic bistro starter, often paired with a crusty baguette. Yet the crunch of the radishes, particularly if they've been perked up in iced water, has little need for a yeasted dough. Instead, try adding the murky flavour of truffle to the combination for a deft bit of distraction. The mushroomy aroma of truffled salt (available from many delis) adds an interesting complexity. If you really want to push the boat out, though, try serving the butter melted with a few slivers of fresh truffle floating and infusing in it.

1 small bunch of radishes (around 8), scrubbed clean and halved
40 g unsalted butter, at room temperature
1 tbsp truffle salt

Soak the radishes in iced water for 10–15 minutes until they are crisp. Dry well before serving.

Present the radishes on a platter with the softened butter in one dish and the truffle salt in another. Encourage guests to swipe a radish half through the butter and then dip it into the truffle salt. No double dipping, please.

FIVE-SPICE SOY ROASTED ALMONDS

Serves 6–8

These are addictive. They're crunchy and salty, sweet and spiced. They remind me of the honey-soy chicken drumsticks my mother used to bake and serve over brown rice on Wednesday nights in 1989. They store perfectly in a Tupperware in the pantry. They pair just as well with a cold ale at 6pm when you walk in the door, as they do with a cup of green tea at 2.30am when you're starving and desperately trying to finish a presentation. And they're a neat way to add a bit of extra crunch to a simple dinner: whether sautéed greens with a soft cooked egg, soy-marinated skirt steak with ribbons of carrot, or even simple baked chicken drumsticks.

250 g almonds
3 tbsp light soy sauce
½ tbsp runny honey or rice malt syrup
2 tsp Chinese five-spice powder
sea salt

Equipment
baking tray lined with baking paper

Preheat the oven to 150°C/300°F/Gas 2.

Spread the almonds in a single layer on the lined baking tray and bake them in the preheated oven for about 10 minutes, or until they smell nutty. Leave the oven on.

Transfer them to a heatproof bowl. Mix together the soy, honey and five-spice powder in a small bowl, then pour it over the almonds. Stir to coat them well.

Transfer the almonds back to the baking tray in a single layer. Bake them again, stirring occasionally, for 15–18 minutes until they are dry and browned.

Taste and season with salt if needed. Serve them warm, or leave them to cool completely before storing in an airtight container.

KALE CRISPS WITH LEMON

Serves 2–4, with drinks

I wanted to hate kale crisps. I wanted to shun them the way I do event television and wedge sneakers. They flamed into the zeitgeist too quickly; they were too faddish; they came from nowhere – like an edible meme – and suddenly they were everywhere, haunting every corner of the internet and wholefood store. But here's the problem: they're very good. They have a pleasant crackle and an elegant texture. And surprisingly for a roasted leaf, they also proved an excellent vehicle for other flavours. You could try them with smoked paprika sprinkled over the top. Cayenne or Sichuan pepper would also be fun. But lemon zest makes them really shine – as though the last thing these crisps needed was anything to draw more of a spotlight onto them.

small bunch of kale, about 200 g, cleaned and
   dried thoroughly
2 tbsp olive oil
grated zest of 1 lemon
sea salt

Equipment
baking tray lined with baking paper

Preheat the oven to 180°C/350°F/Gas 4.

Pull the tendrils of the kale away from the hard stems and discard the stems. Gently tear the tendrils into pieces around the size of a Pringle.

Scatter the kale in a single layer over the lined baking tray. You may have to do this in batches. Drizzle the kale with the olive oil, and sprinkle with the lemon zest and some salt, to taste.

Roast the kale in the preheated oven until mostly crisp – 10–13 minutes. If it's browning too much, turn some of the leaves over. A word of caution: if you take them to the browner edge, they will taste more roasted and a little more bitter.

Allow the kale to cool completely before storing in an airtight container.

PADRÓN PEPPERS WITH JAMÓN SALT

Serves 4

It just makes sense that these two things should be joined together. It's a rare occasion that a bowl of blistered pimientos de Padrón isn't followed by a platter of cured meats. These small peppers hailing from northwest Spain are both a grand starter and a gamble – anywhere between five and 20 per cent of them will be blazingly hot. You can try and guess which ones they will be, but really, the best way is to suck them and see.

For those who don't fancy cured meat in their salt, feel free to season the peppers liberally with just Maldon salt flakes, or the salt flakes combined with some smoked paprika or lemon zest.

20 g jamón
1 tbsp sea salt flakes
1 tbsp olive oil
300 g padrón peppers

To make the jamón salt, put the jamón in a saucepan and cook it over medium heat until it is crisp. Remove it from the pan and leave it to cool.

Put the cooled jamón in a food processor and blitz to make fine crumbs, then mix them with the salt flakes. Alternatively, grind it with the salt using a pestle and mortar. Set aside.

To cook the peppers, heat the olive oil in a deep frying pan over medium heat. When the oil is shimmering, add the peppers.

Cook and stir the peppers until their skins are brown and blistered. Careful – they may spit.

Remove the peppers from the pan, place on a plate and sprinkle with the jamón salt, to taste.

EDAMAME WITH BROWN RICE TEA SALT

Serves 4

I doubt at this stage whether anyone needs any instruction on how to eat edamame, those immature soybeans in pods that have become a ubiquitous starter at most Japanese restaurants and sushi-go-arounds. But just in case, here's a hint. Don't eat the case. It's leathery and tough and as unpalatable as can be. And you'll look a little like a numpty. Instead, transfer the pod directly to your mouth and use your teeth to extract each bean. Lightly steamed or boiled, these beans are naturally sweet – a little sprinkling of salt is what really makes them sing. And for a nifty twist, try muddling your salt with some brown rice tea. It offers a smokey depth that makes for a compelling slow-carb snack.

1 tbsp sea salt flakes
1 tea bag of Japanese brown rice tea (genmaicha),
  or a green tea bag
500 g frozen edamame in their pods

Mix together the sea salt and the contents of the brown rice tea bag.

Bring a saucepan of water to the boil. Add the frozen edamame and cook for about 4 minutes, or until the pods turn bright green and are heated through. Drain them and transfer them to a large bowl. Toss them with the brown rice tea salt and serve them with a bowl to the side for the empty casings.

PIGS IN KIMCHEE BLANKETS

Serves 4

You might not think that spicy, fermented Korean cabbage, twee sausages, a sweet glaze and a downy tuft of Parmesan cheese would be friends. You may, in fact, think that I'm mad for clumping them together on a cocktail stick. But please, trust me here. Pigs in blankets on their own – that cocktail staple and barnyard coupling of sausage with a coat of cured pig or pastry – is too much. Too much meat, too much fat; too one-dimensional in its notes of squish and salt. Here it gets taken out for a spin by two exotic friends, and is all the better for it. The kimchee adds a kooky layer of acidity and spice. The rice-malt glaze gives a sweet shine and the Parmesan provides the final twirl of complexity – an umami roundness that takes it to the next level completely. Essentially, what you're looking at are the core ingredients in the most hipster of hotdogs, bar the bread, which I think most of us will agree can be the most boring bit of all.

8 rashers of bacon, trimmed to 10 cm long and 3 cm wide
160 g kimchee
8 good-quality chipolata sausages.
1½ tbsp rice malt syrup or pure maple syrup
30 g Parmesan, finely grated

Equipment
8 cocktail sticks
baking tray lined with baking paper

Preheat the oven to 180°C/350°F/Gas 4.

Lay out the rashers of bacon and cover each one with a dollop of kimchee.

Swaddle each raw chipolata in kimchee and bacon, with the bacon outermost. Thread a cocktail stick through the bacon to fasten it closed and pin it to the sausage.

Arrange the blanketed pigs on the lined baking tray and brush them with the syrup. Bake them in the preheated oven for 30–35 minutes, until the bacon is brown and the sausages are piping hot.

Sprinkle the Parmesan over the pigs in blankets just before serving with napkins – and possibly a cold ale or two.

QUINOA AND COURGETTE FRITTERS WITH STRAINED YOGHURT

Makes 12–14

These natty vegetarian and gluten-free fritters are as happy on a tray with drinks while you watch the sun slip down with a crowd of six, as they are at a breakfast for two. There are so many winning aspects – from the earthiness of the grated courgettes to the sparkle of salt from the olive tapenade. Then there are the quinoa flakes which offer both protein and the body to bind them together. They're delightful with strained yoghurt or feta cheese crumbled over the top but they are also sterling with some smoked salmon or a poached egg if what you're really after is a substantial supper for one.

2 medium courgettes, grated
100 g rolled quinoa flakes
60 ml milk
4 tbsp olive tapenade
a pinch of dried chilli flakes (optional)
2 eggs, lightly beaten
15 fresh mint leaves, very finely chopped
handful of fresh flat-leaf parsley leaves, very finely chopped
1 spring onion, diced
1 tsp sea salt
4 tbsp olive oil
chilli sauce (optional)

To serve
300 g Greek yoghurt and 1 tsp sea salt; chilli sauce (optional)

Stir together the courgettes, quinoa flakes, milk, tapenade, chilli flakes, eggs, mint, parsley, spring onion and salt until well combined.

Put half of the olive oil in a non-stick frying pan. Drop in 1 tablespoon of batter per fritter and fry until golden on the bottom. You can probably do 3–4 at a time. Use a spatula or fish slice to gently flip the fritters over, then cook the other sides until the outsides are crisp and the fritters hold together. Keep them warm in a low oven while you make the remaining fritters using the remaining oil to grease the pan.

To serve, season the yoghurt with the salt and dollop on the fritters, perhaps with some chilli sauce on the side.

TIP: *These can be made ahead and frozen in Tupperware between slips of baking paper; just reinvigorate them in the oven, a pan or toasted sandwich press.*

ROASTED AND FRESH TOMATO SKEWERS WITH MINT AND HALLOUMI

Serves 4

Snacks on cocktail sticks have a certain retro whimsy. These starters follow that lead, but with a modern twist; no cheddar or pineapple chunks here, thanks. Instead you'll find that tomato with mint and sheep's milk cheese form a cracking combination – sweet and acidic, fresh and milky all at once. Halloumi can occasionally have the texture of a kitchen sponge, particularly when it's overcooked. The key is to grill it over a blazing surface just long enough for the outside to caramelise and the interior to relax. Check if your surface is hot enough by placing half a lemon, cut side down, on it. If it sizzles on contact, you're right to start cooking. Once the skewers are done, you'll have a ready-made dressing in the blistered lemons: winner.

16 cherry tomatoes, halved
3 tbsp olive oil
a pinch of sea salt
1 lemon, halved
180 g halloumi cheese, cut horizontally into 1-cm thick slices
16 fresh mint leaves

Equipment
16 cocktail sticks

Preheat the oven to 180°C/350°F/Gas 4.

Place half of the tomatoes, cut side up, in a baking dish and drizzle with 1 tablespoon of the olive oil, and the salt. Bake them in the preheated oven for 20 minutes, or until the tops have started to blister and soften.

Five minutes before the tomatoes are ready, heat the remaining olive oil in a non-stick frying pan over medium heat. Test when the pan is hot enough by placing the 2 lemon halves, cut side down, in the pan. When they sizzle, it's time to add the halloumi slices. Leave the lemon where it is and add the halloumi. Fry it for 2–3 minutes on each side until it has developed a mottled brown tan. The lemon should also have caramelised, creating an instant dressing for the halloumi.

Drain the halloumi on kitchen paper, then cut each slice into 8 pieces the size of a postage stamp. Skewer onto a cocktail stick a piece of halloumi, a roasted tomato half, a mint leaf and a fresh tomato half. Serve them hot, with the blistered lemon halves on the side to squeeze over.

ARTICHOKES WITH RED-EYE AÏOLI

Serves 4

A whole artichoke is hospitality in a nutshell, clubbing together in one neat package both your centrepiece and appetiser. Next time you have guests over in spring – when artichokes are at their best – consider steaming a whole beauty and allow your guests to collectively pull off frond after frond, scraping the curved bases lazily against their lower teeth to extract every scratch of flesh. You could join it with a simple vinaigrette of olive oil, Dijon mustard and red wine vinegar for dipping. Or you could take a cue from the American South, a place that has perfected the art of hosting. This red-eye aïoli takes its inspiration from the classic southern red-eye gravy, which uses the depth and smokiness of coffee to counterpoint the saltiness of ham and bacon. It's a notion that applies just as well to a steamed and seasoned artichoke. Muddle the red eye aïoli ('red eye-oli') together, put it on a platter with the artichoke and don't forget a bowl for the discarded leaves. If, despite all your best efforts to make things convivial, conversation flails, rest assured you can always play the game of 'guess the secret ingredient in the sauce'.

1 large artichoke
1 fresh or dried bay leaf
½ lemon
hot water, to cover

Red-eye aïoli
1 egg yolk
100 ml sunflower oil
1 small garlic cloves, grated
2 tsp espresso at room temperature
a good pinch of sea salt
1 tsp lemon juice

To cook the artichoke, first cut off the top couple of centimetres where the leaves are tightly bunched, like a bud. Also trim the stem to just 2 cm in length. If the sharp points of the remaining leaves are particularly spiky, you can trim them too (or just be careful while you eat it not to stab yourself).

Put the artichoke in a large pot and pour in enough hot water to come three-quarters of the way up the artichoke. Add the bay leaf and lemon and clamp a lid on the pot. Bring the water to the boil, then lower the heat so that the water is just simmering. Simmer for 25–45 minutes or until you can easily pull the outer leaves off.

For the aïoli
Place a wet tea towel under a clean bowl (this will help make the bowl more stable). Whisk the egg yolk for 30 seconds to help get some air into it.

Very slowly trickle a small amount of oil down the side of the bowl. Whisk until it has emulsified with the egg yolk. Do this again. And again and again. Do not pour freely until you have a good, thick and glossy-looking mayonnaise. If you've split the mayonnaise and it won't take the oil, don't throw out what you have. Just get a fresh bowl and crack another egg yolk into it. Now trickle the oil/egg mixture in, bit by bit. When that has turned into a mayonnaise, add the remaining oil.

When you're satisfied with your mayonnaise, turn it into the red-eye aïoli by adding the garlic and coffee. Stir, then season generously with salt. Taste. If you think it needs more, add more salt to help balance the flavours.

Serve the warm artichoke in the middle of the table and let people pull off leaves and dunk the bases in the aïoli.

SPICED CHICKPEA BOMBS

Serves 4

Who knew that chickpeas, when roasted in a little bit of olive oil, turn into crisp balls which shatter like your favourite party mix? If you did – well done. If not, do try these. They're simple to make and the perfect thing to lay out with a stiff drink at the end of a long day. I like them with a bit of a spicy kick but if you prefer a milder flavour, omit the cayenne and perhaps add some ground cinnamon or ginger for a more romantic lilt. The best thing about these is that I bet all the ingredients are in your cupboard, most of the time. So if you get stuck having people over and need something nifty to serve, a novel thing to pick at is only 30 minutes away.

1 x 400-g tin of chickpeas, rinsed and dried thoroughly
3 tbsp olive oil
½–1 tbsp ground cayenne pepper (depending on how spicy you like things)
1 tbsp ground cumin
1 tbsp ground coriander
1 tsp sea salt

Equipment
baking tray lined with baking paper

Preheat the oven to 190°C/375°F/Gas 5.

Scatter the chickpeas over the lined baking tray in a single layer.

Mix together the olive oil, cayenne, cumin and coriander in a small bowl, then scatter it over the chickpeas. Stir to coat them well.

Bake the chickpeas in the preheated oven for about 20 minutes.

Shake the tray a little to move the chickpeas around and allow all the surfaces to get some heat from the oven. Return the tray to the oven for another 15 minutes until the chickpeas are crispy.

Remove the tray from the oven, sprinkle the chickpeas with the salt and leave them to cool before eating or storing them in an airtight container.

COURGETTE FRITES

Serves 4–6

You can get lofty and call them frites but really, fries are fries. They're slivers of vegetable, cooked in oil until crisp, then seasoned and consumed – often by the fistful. They're what you want as a side to a steak. They're perfect dabbed in mustard alongside a roast chicken. And they shouldn't be constrained to starches. These frites are a little lighter than their potato-based cousin. Courgettes offer a yielding centre while the chickpea flour and soda water in the batter crisp up beautifully. Granted, these are not everyday food, so treat them as an exotic visitor and dust them in za'atar, a blend of oregano, thyme and sesame. Spritz them with lemon. Maybe dip them in yoghurt and tahini. Then savour every hot, salty bite.

75 g chickpea (besan or gram) flour
½ tsp baking powder
½ tsp freshly ground black pepper
½ tbsp ground coriander
1 egg yolk, whisked
½ tbsp vegetable oil
125 ml soda water
3 medium courgettes, cut into 1-cm batons
1 tbsp table salt
500–750 ml vegetable oil, for frying
1½ tbsp za'atar

Whisk together the flour, baking powder, pepper and coriander in a large bowl. Drizzle the egg yolk and the ½ tablespoon of oil into the bowl and use a fork to create a craggy dough. Slowly pour in the soda water, whisking continuously until a smooth batter forms. Cover with clingfilm and refrigerate for at least 1 hour.

When you are ready to fry the frites, heat the oil for frying in a large saucepan until it reaches 190°C/375°F on a cooking thermometer. If you don't have a thermometer, the oil is ready when a cube of bread dropped into it browns in 30 seconds.

Take a handful of courgette batons, drop them into the batter and make sure they're well coated. Use tongs to gently lower them into the hot oil and fry them until they're golden – about 4 minutes. Remove them from the oil with a slotted spoon and drain them on kitchen paper. Allow the oil to return to 190°C/375°F and repeat the process with the remaining batons and batter.

Sprinkle the frites with the salt and za'atar before serving. If you fancy a condiment, then plain yoghurt muddled with some olive oil and lemon juice works well.

There are few things more comforting than a good bowl of soup. I'm not talking about meek broths. I'm talking about chunky, hearty bowls of sustenance. The sort which, while you eat them with a spoon, keeping a fork nearby won't seem like complete folly.

Most of what follows makes a perfect swift lunch; portioned into sandwich bags and frozen, it also makes excellent back-up suppers on cold nights when you need to be warmed from the inside out. In winter it's a rare week when there's not a simmering pot of the ultimate ham and lentil soup, or ribollita on the stove. On those steaming summer eves when it's too hot to think let alone cook, I take comfort in knowing that I can have a cooling bowl of white bean, cucumber, mint and yoghurt, or curried chickpea soup in a bowl in less time than it takes to soften an onion. And if I'm feeling poorly, nothing fails to bring me back from the brink like the 'all the Nanas' chicken, lemon, egg and white bean soup', though the quinoa aguadito with its perky strains of coriander and lime comes a close second.

SOUPS (A DIFFERENT KIND OF LIQUID LUNCH)

ALL THE NANAS' CHICKEN, LEMON, EGG AND WHITE BEAN SOUP

Serves 2

This soup came to me when I called on the wisdom of all the Nanas I know to bring me back from the brink of a terrible cold. There's chicken stock, poached chicken, carrot and celery – the necessary base of all restorative soups. There's a slight Asian lilt from the garlic and chilli. There are beans for sustenance. And in the spirit of Greek avgolemono the lemon and beaten egg added at the end evolve into a gentle spider web of protein through the bowl. To save this dish just for days when you're poorly, though, would be a waste. It also tastes grand when you're at your best but someone close to you needs a little helping hand.

2 chicken breasts
1 small red chilli, deseeded and diced
1 carrot, peeled and finely diced
1 rib of celery, finely diced
625 ml good-quality chicken stock (homemade is best)
1 x 400-g tin of white beans, rinsed
2 eggs, beaten
1 lemon, quartered
handful of fresh flat-leaf parsley leaves, chopped
sea salt and freshly ground black pepper

Put the chicken breasts, chilli, carrot and celery in a saucepan with the chicken stock over medium heat. Bring the stock up to a simmer and poach the contents until the chicken is cooked through and shreds easily – about 10–15 minutes. Remove the chicken from the pan, shred it with 2 forks and divide it between 2 soup bowls. Reserve the pan with its contents.

Divide the beans between the bowls with the chicken.

Pour the beaten egg into the pan with the simmering chicken stock and vegetables and keep the pan over medium heat, stirring until the egg collects in threads.

Season the soup with salt, pepper and lemon juice. You want the soup to have personality. Divide the soup between the soup bowls and top with chopped parsley and another lemon cheek.

ULTIMATE HAM
AND LENTIL SOUP

Serves 4–6

There is very little that is sexy about lentil soup. Yet like many frumpy things (flight socks, dental floss, flesh-toned underwear etc), it's incredibly useful. It makes a sturdy lunch; it freezes beautifully; and it's a soup that actually works for supper. All it needs is a couple of tricks to transform it into a shining staple. Firstly, try to beg off your local deli their jamón or prosciutto ends – they offer a depth of flavour far beyond what you'd get from a ham bone (while also avoiding the unsightly jellification you'll get from hock). The other trick is to include diced nori strips – while there is little that's Japanese about this dish, the seaweed plays in the same umami key as the jamón, melting into the soup and making it earthy, savoury, and utterly delicious.

300 g green or brown lentils (or a mix of both)
1 tbsp olive oil
1 onion, peeled and diced
1 carrot, peeled and finely diced
2 fresh or dried bay leaves
300 g jamón or prosciutto ends, cut into pieces the size of
   a matchbox (be sure to trim off any large sections of fat
   and remove any twine or plastic that's sneakily sticking out)
2 litres vegetable stock
2 tbsp nori strips

To serve
grated zest and juice of ½ lemon, and olive oil

Soak the lentils in a bowl of cold water for 1 hour, then drain and discard the water.

Add the olive oil to a heavy-based saucepan or casserole dish over medium heat. Add the onion and carrot and sauté for 5–7 minutes until softened. Add the lentils, bay leaves, chunky jamón or prosciutto ends, vegetable stock and nori and bring to the boil.

Reduce the heat and simmer, covered with a lid, for 1–2 hours, until the lentils have broken down and the jamón or prosciutto has imparted a savoury flavour.

Remove the jamón or prosciutto and bay leaves from the soup and use a balloon whisk to encourage some of the lentils to break down further. Shred the ham with 2 forks if you can and return it to the pan to mix it in. Portion the soup into bowls. Brighten it up with a little lemon zest and juice and a glug of olive oil.

TIP: *The inclusion of the seaweed in this soup helps to mollify the trumpeting potential side effects of a large bowl of pulses.*

TURKISH RED LENTIL SOUP

Serves 6

Red lentil soup can rescue you from anything, whether it's a crummy morning marred by parking tickets, or torrential Turkish rain en route to the Aya Sofia just before you discover it's closed for the day. This soup is a balance of excitement and comfort, with the smooth texture of the lentils playing second fiddle to the thrum of cumin and the trilling of sumac, that berry-red and slightly sour spice. This makes a terrific vegetarian supper on its own perhaps with some Swiss chard or kale stirred through at the end. But if you're the sort of person who needs some meat for a meal to feel complete, a few browned lamb meatballs bobbing around in the bottom of the bowl won't go astray.

1½ tbsp ground cumin
3 tbsp olive oil
2 red onions, peeled and finely diced
2 garlic cloves, minced or finely diced
2 carrots, peeled and diced
3 tbsp tomato paste
500 g red lentils, washed
1.25 litres water
sea salt

To serve
3 tbsp labneh (strained Greek yoghurt)
small bunch of fresh mint leaves, torn
3 tsp sumac
chilli, finely shredded kale or browned lamb meatballs
  (all optional)

Put the cumin in a heavy-based saucepan or casserole dish over medium heat. Toast for 1 minute or until it smells nutty, then pour in the oil.

Add the onions, garlic and carrots and sauté for about 5–7 minutes until they have softened. Add the tomato paste and stir to combine.

Add the lentils, pour in the water and bring it to the boil. Once it has boiled, turn the heat down to bring the liquid to a simmer and cover the pan with the lid. Cook for 20–25 minutes, until the lentils have broken down, stirring occasionally to prevent anything from catching on the bottom of the pan.

Add ½ tablespoon sea salt, turn off the heat and leave with the lid on for another 5–10 minutes.

Using a stick blender or food processor, blend the soup until smooth. Check the seasoning and add more salt to taste.

Serve the soup with a splodge of labneh, fresh mint leaves and a good sprinkling of sumac. Chilli, kale and meatballs are all optional.

RIBOLLITA

Serves 4–6

A true Tuscan ribollita is bulked out with stale bread. This is not that soup. In fact, it's probably a stretch even claiming it a member of its extended family. But whatever its moniker, this is definitely a worthy dish for your winter repertoire. It's rustic and filling with blended beans and tastes surprisingly complex courtesy of the sneaky inclusion of a Parmesan rind in the stock. For a meat-free version, omit the lardons and replace the chicken stock with vegetable. But it's best not to overlook the pesto at the end – it will keep well in the fridge covered in some olive oil and elevates this rough and ready stew from a homely dish to something I'd happily serve up to company, any day of the week.

If you are serving it to guests, think about following it up with something equally hearty but slightly more refined, like the Orange, Chocolate and Hazelnut Puddings on page 170.

1 tbsp olive oil
100 g lardons or streaky bacon cut into batons
1 tbsp fennel seeds
1 red onion, peeled and diced
2 carrots, peeled and diced
½ fennel bulb, diced
3 garlic cloves, peeled and thinly sliced
½–1 tsp dried chilli flakes
2 x 400-g tins of cannellini beans, rinsed
750 ml chicken stock
1 Parmesan rind
200 g cavolo nero or kale, leaves and stalks thinly sliced
sea salt and freshly ground black pepper

Rocket, lemon and walnut pesto
large handful of baby rocket
grated zest of ½ lemon
½ garlic clove
2 tbsp chopped walnuts
25 g grated Parmesan
60 ml olive oil

Heat the olive oil in a heavy-based saucepan or casserole dish over medium heat. Add the lardons and fennel seeds and sauté until the lardon fat begins to render. Add the onion, carrots, fennel, garlic and chilli flakes and sauté over low–medium heat for 10–12 minutes until the vegetables have started to soften.

Tip one tin of rinsed beans into a food processor with the chicken stock and blitz to a purée. Add the liquid to the pan along with the other tin of whole beans and the Parmesan rind. Simmer, covered with the lid, for 30 minutes.

After 30 minutes, add the cavolo nero or kale and simmer, uncovered, for 10 minutes to soften.

To make the rocket, lemon and walnut pesto, blend all the ingredients together in a food processor until smooth. Taste and season with salt and pepper.

Remove the Parmesan rind from the soup. Portion into bowls and serve with a generous dollop of the pesto on top.

ROAST BLOODY MARY TOMATO SOUP

Serves 4

There are things you miss, both while growing a small person inside of you and in the aftermath of trying to feed them off your own body. For me, Bloody Marys were chief among them. That sprightly combination of tomato juice, vodka, Worcestershire and Tabasco with a swizzle stick of celery is downright celebratory and a hallmark of a good time on any side of the horizon. It was from those unfulfilled cravings that this virgin version was born, substituting the warmth from the booze for some time in the oven. Both the celery and tomatoes become deepened and softened after a spell and the roast garlic adds a surprising sweetness. The white beans are optional, but they do help make it more substantial, without interrupting the flavour profile too much. The only thing to be careful of is the amount of heat you add. The second time I made this I turned up the volume, savouring the burn. Two hours later I fed my six-week-old son. Sometimes a Bloody Mary can keep you up all night for good reasons. This was not one. In the hours that followed, my son fussed and fretted, spilled and complained, until I finally clocked that not everyone likes things to be searingly hot. So learn from my mistakes and proceed with caution; you can always add more spice, but once it's there, it can be rather hard to take it away.

1 whole garlic bulb with the top lopped off
250 g celery (or 3 ribs) cut into sticks 6 cm long
 (leafy ends reserved for serving)
800 g (or 10–12) ripe Roma tomatoes, halved lengthways
4 tbsp olive oil
2 tsp sea salt
1–2 tsp dried chilli flakes (depending on how hot you
 like things)
1 x 400-g tin of white beans, rinsed
2 tbsp Worcestershire sauce
juice of ½ lemon
125 ml water
Tabasco, to taste

Preheat the oven to 150°C/300°F/Gas 2.

Put the garlic, celery and Roma tomatoes, cut side up, on a baking tray. Drizzle with the olive oil and sprinkle with the salt and chilli flakes. Roast them in the preheated oven for 1½ hours or until the tomatoes have puckered. Allow them to cool for 5–10 minutes.

Squeeze the roasted garlic cloves out of their casings and add them to a food processor or blender with the roasted vegetables and any juices from the baking tray. Add the beans, Worcestershire, lemon juice and water and blend until smooth. Taste and season with extra salt, chilli or lemon juice, if required.

Serve the soup hot with the celery ends for dipping and Tabasco for those who want an extra kick.

TIP: *If you fancy a bit more protein you can also transform this into a 'red eye' with a poached egg floating in the centre.*

CHILLED WHITE BEAN, CUCUMBER, MINT AND YOGHURT SOUP

Serves 1–2

There are days when it's too hot to think, let alone cook. When those occasions of sweltering summer descend, this what I turn to. It's not quite a gazpacho and it's not quite tzatziki. There's a streak of garlic and lemon for zing, the floral softness of cucumber, the body of white beans and the lightness of yoghurt. If you're after something refined, strain it before serving and take care with the placement of the olives, mint leaves and pistachios. If you're merely hot and hungry, whizz it until it's as smooth as you think it will go and portion it straight into bowls, leaving the adornments out on the table for everyone to fix themselves.

½ telegraph (large) cucumber
1x 400-g tin of white beans, rinsed
grated zest and juice of ½ lemon
300 g Greek yoghurt
1 small garlic clove, peeled and grated
handful of fresh mint leaves
1 ice cube
1 tbsp olive oil, plus extra to drizzle
sea salt and freshly ground black pepper
handful of shelled pistachios
handful of green olives, pitted and sliced
green chilli, diced (optional)

Grate the cucumber into a bowl and add the beans, lemon zest and juice, yoghurt, garlic and three-quarters of the mint leaves.

Blitz the ingredients in the bowl with a stick blender or in a food processor until they are all combined and well blended. Add the ice cube and allow it to melt and chill the soup down.

If you prefer a smoother, more elegant soup, now strain it through a strainer.

Season the soup with salt, pepper and the olive oil, then portion it into bowls. Top with the remaining mint, the pistachios and olives and a drizzle more of olive oil, if needed. Add some chilli for heat, if liked.

CHILLED CURRIED CHICKPEA SOUP

Serves 1 generously, or 2 modestly

This soup takes all of the warmth from a chickpea curry and makes it palatable for those days when the bitumen burns the bottom of your feet. It pairs perfectly with a frosty ale and a sporting match you're only half interested in seeing the outcome of. Don't be tempted to scrimp on the turmeric chickpeas – they provide a delightful contrast of textures (though if you were pushed for time you could always lob on top a few of the Spiced Chickpea Bombs from page 44).

1 x 400-g tin of chickpeas, rinsed
200 g cherry tomatoes
¾ tbsp curry powder
1 lime
4 tbsp Greek yoghurt
4 ice cubes
2 tbsp sunflower oil
1 tsp ground turmeric
small green or red chilli, diced

Equipment
a blender that can crush ice cubes

Blend three-quarters of the chickpeas, all the cherry tomatoes and curry powder, the juice and zest of ½ the lime, 2 tbsp of the Greek yoghurt and the ice cubes until smooth. If it is too chunky, add a couple of tablespoons of cold water. Chill the soup in the fridge until serving.

Heat the oil and turmeric in a frying pan. Fry the remaining chickpeas until golden and crisp.

If you prefer a smoother, more elegant soup, now strain it through a strainer.

Portion the soup into bowls. Top with a swirl of the remaining yoghurt, a wedge of lime, the chilli and the turmeric chickpeas.

QUINOA AGUADITO, OR PERUVIAN CHICKEN AND CORIANDER SOUP

Serves 2–3

This is not a soup for that portion of the population who thinks coriander tastes unspeakably like soap. But for the rest of us, it can be something of a revelation. The first time a Peruvian friend made me aguadito, I was floored by the quantity of green fronds that found their way into the pot. It was bold and brash and something to behold, particularly the way the strong taste of coriander was anchored by the silkiness of chicken stock and zip of lime and chilli. And while the flavours may appear all light and bright, this is a soup that's deceptively filling, particularly if you take the liberties that I have by inserting green peas and quinoa. Quinoa isn't traditional in an aguadito, but to me it's a natural inclusion – clutching two of Peru's most famed tastes together in a single bowl.

large bunch of fresh coriander, well washed
1 onion
2 garlic cloves, peeled
3 tbsp olive oil
1 litre chicken stock
85 g quinoa, rinsed well
130 g frozen peas
2 raw chicken breasts or 350 g cooked chicken, shredded
1 tsp sea salt

To serve
2–3 lime wedges and finely chopped green chilli (optional)

To prepare the coriander, trim the very ends off the stems. Now roughly chop the stems and set the leaves aside for later.

Put the coriander stems, onion, garlic and 2 tablespoons of the olive oil in a food processor and blitz to a paste.

Place a saucepan over medium heat. Add the coriander paste and fry for about 3 minutes to soften the onion and garlic.

Add the chicken stock to the pan and bring it to the boil. Add the quinoa, cover the pan with the lid and simmer for 15 minutes. If you are using raw chicken, place it in the pot now to poach. After 15 minutes, or when the quinoa and chicken are cooked through, remove the chicken from the pan and shred it with 2 forks.

Add the frozen peas and shredded chicken to the pan and heat until the peas and chicken are piping hot.

Pound the reserved coriander leaves, the remaining olive oil and the salt together to a paste either using a pestle and mortar or a food processor. Stir this through the soup before serving it with lime wedges and if you fancy things to be a little hotter, green chilli, to taste.

AJO BLANCO
WITH RED GRAPES

Serves 4

This is another soup traditionally bolstered with bread (this time from the south of Spain) which finds a new life with the inclusion of beans. The silky emulsion of blanched almonds, poached garlic and infused milk is traditionally served cold with slivered grapes for sweetness. Green are classic, but the contrast of the red is what floats my boat. It also makes an elegant amuse-bouche in shot glasses, perhaps with pearls of pomegranate festooned on top; and by omitting the water it will also make a terrific warm sauce for roast fish, lamb or chicken (try it with the seabass on page 90). In order to get the right velvety smooth texture you will need a powerful blender, or if it's still a bit chunky, strain it before serving.

3 garlic cloves, peeled
250 ml milk
120 g blanched almonds
½ x 400-g tin of cannellini beans, rinsed
1 tsp sea salt
125 ml water
2 tbsp olive oil
1 tsp red wine vinegar
12 red grapes, cut into slivers

Put the garlic and milk in a saucepan over low–medium heat and bring to a simmer. Poach the garlic for about 7 minutes, or until the point of a knife can slide easily through it.

Put the infused milk, poached garlic, almonds, beans and salt into a powerful blender or food processor. Blend until you have a paste. Drizzle in the water and continue to blend until you have a smooth, creamy consistency.

Drizzle in the olive oil and vinegar and blend to emulsify.

Serve the soup either lukewarm or chilled, with red grape slivers floating on the top of each portion.

GREEN SOUP WITH CHORIZO ALMOND CRUMBS

Serves 2–3

The nights when you crave something green often emerge from the pale plateau of jet lag. This soup's origins follow a late flight from Sydney. When I asked The Hungry One what he fancied for dinner, the answer was: 'I should probably eat something green. But I'm a little too tired to chew'. So that's how this Kermit-hued pot of joy was born. Here are a few guiding principles to help steer the course: treat the vegetables the same as if you were making a stir-fry (chop them roughly the same size so the cooking is quick and consistent); start sautéing the hardier ingredients before the delicate ones and don't overcook them; douse everything briefly in piping hot stock and remove it from the hob before it turns as brown and grim as a bunch of forgotten flowers.

You may question the inclusion of apple, but it does help to temper the bitterness of the brassicas. As for the chorizo and almonds – they're there just for a little spice and contrast but if you're keen on a vegetarian route, you can top it with some goats' curd, lemon zest and toasted pine nuts and you'll find it's just as restorative (if not even more so).

1 tbsp olive oil
1 sweet red apple, peeled, cored and diced
200 g (6 stems) tenderstem broccoli/broccolini, diced – including stems (you could also substitute with ½ head of broccoli)
1 courgette, diced
220 g frozen peas
3 handfuls of kale, finely chopped
500 ml hot vegetable or chicken stock
sea salt
2 tbsp fresh flat-leaf parsley leaves

Chorizo crumble (optional)
50 g chorizo, crumbled by hand into small pieces
1–2 tbsp olive oil and 1 tsp smoked paprika, if needed
2 tbsp flaked almonds

Heat the olive oil in a heavy-based saucepan or casserole dish over medium heat. Add the apple and sauté for 2 minutes. Add the broccoli and sauté for 2–4 minutes until it begins to soften.

Add the courgette, peas and kale and sauté for about 4 minutes, stirring so the peas defrost and the kale wilts.

Pour the hot stock into the pan and bring it to a simmer. Cover the pan with the lid and simmer until the apple and broccoli are soft.

Using a stick blender, food processor or blender, blitz the contents of the pan until smooth. If you are using a food processor or blender, be careful – don't fill it all the way to the top and be sure to place a tea towel over the top of the blender while you blitz, as hot liquids can expand and spill out.

Taste and season with salt if needed.

To make the optional chorizo crumble, fry the chorizo in a frying pan over medium heat until it is cooked through and has leached crimson oil into the pan. If there is none, then add the olive oil and smoked paprika. Add the flaked almonds and cook until the almonds have been toasted in the oil.

Serve the soup with the chorizo crumble and parsley scattered over the top.

If not a baked potato, then what? If not fluffy naan, boiled rice, hot chips, velvety mash, or an artful twirl of noodles, then what will occupy the lion's share of your dinner plate? The following are a collection of sides and salads that now take pride of place on our table. I'll often match one with a variety of simply grilled and roasted proteins, from slow-roasted lamb, to quickly grilled chicken skewers, a seared piece of steak or salmon, a square of steamed tofu or a five-minute egg. They're worldly and fun, swift – and best yet – filling, made from either smart carbs, vegetables or some sneaky protein. All of which means I've finally reached a stage where I can put a piece of grilled fish and one of the following on the table for dinner and The Hungry One will no longer look around and wonder what's for the main course.

INTERESTING SIDES & SALADS (FILLING ENOUGH TO FEED A 6'3" MAN)

SIMPLE PURÉES AS A BASE FOR PROTEIN (BYE BYE MASHED POTATO!)

It's the pliant squish of white carbs I found hardest to live without. What is a lamb cutlet without a bed of mashed potatoes, an osso bucco without a base of risotto Milanese, or a tagine without a downy tumble of couscous on the side?

One easy solution can be found in purées of other, lower-GI vegetables and pulses. Simply steamed, wilted or warmed through then blitzed with a stick blender, these six purées swiftly become simple building blocks for sturdy meals. Once you've got the basics mastered, all that's needed are some extra spices or herbs to twist them in an entirely new direction (try cumin or turmeric with the carrot, or mint or tarragon with the peas). And if your inspiration and inclination to cook start and end with a purée, never fear – slosh in an extra cup of water or stock and you've got yourself a bowl of soup. Dinner: sorted.

FENNEL PURÉE

Serves 2

1 tsp fennel seeds
4 tbsp olive oil
1 medium fennel bulb (or 2 small ones),
  root and tips trimmed, diced
a pinch of sea salt

Add the fennel seeds to a dry frying pan over medium heat and cook for 1–2 minutes, shaking frequently. Add half of the olive oil, the fennel and salt and sauté for 7–10 minutes until the fennel has softened. Purée with the remaining olive oil until smooth.

TO SERVE: *Great as a base for fish or pork. With pork, try adding a peeled, cored and diced Granny Smith apple to the pan.*

CAULIFLOWER PURÉE

Serves 6 (and freezes well)

1 head of cauliflower, green bits discarded,
  cut into small florets and stem diced
250 ml water
a pinch of sea salt
2 tbsp olive oil

Put the cauliflower and water in a saucepan and bring to a simmer. Cover the pan with the lid and cook at a gentle simmer over medium heat for 15 minutes, stirring occasionally to prevent it catching or scorching. After 15 minutes, remove the lid and simmer for another 10 minutes, stirring occasionally until the cauliflower is soft. Purée with the salt and olive oil until smooth.

TO SERVE: *Shines when paired with steak, sausages, chicken, scallops or roast lamb, or try it on its own with some herb oil or pesto drizzled over the top for a warming soup.*

PEA PURÉE

Serves 2

260 g frozen peas
1½ tbsp water
1 tbsp olive oil
½ tsp sea salt

Put the peas and water in a saucepan over medium heat until the peas are hot through. Purée with the olive oil and salt and serve warm.

TO SERVE: *Lovely with pink fish, chicken or lamb. Try adding a handful of fresh mint and a tablespoon of crumbled feta or a tablespoon of pesto. Alternatively, fry a tablespoon of green curry paste in the pan before adding the peas for a refreshing Asian alternative to rice alongside a whole baked fish.*

CARROT PURÉE

Serves 2

4 medium carrots, peeled and diced
1 tbsp olive oil
½ tsp sea salt

Steam the carrots for 2 minutes or until they can be pierced with the tip of a knife. Purée with the olive oil and salt. Serve warm.

TO SERVE: *Terrific with roast beef, chicken or white fish. Try adding 3 tablespoons hummus or 1 tablespoon tahini for a Middle Eastern turn, or fresh, grated ginger for a bit of zip.*

WHITE BEAN PURÉE

Serves 4

2 x 400-g tins of cannellini beans, rinsed
1½ tbsp milk
1 tbsp olive oil
½ tsp salt

Blitz together the beans and milk using a stick blender or food processor, until smooth. Transfer the purée to a saucepan and gently heat, stirring often to prevent it from sticking to the pan. Season with salt and drizzle with olive oil just before serving.

TO SERVE: *Use whenever you would use mashed potato. Try adding roast garlic, or folding through kale and spring onion for a take on colcannon (see page 142).*

SPLIT PEA PURÉE

Serves 4

210 g dried yellow split peas, rinsed
1 fresh or dried bay leaf
3 garlic cloves, peeled
1 tsp sea salt
4 tbsp extra virgin olive oil
2 tbsp good-quality red wine vinegar

Put the split peas in a large saucepan over high heat and add enough cold water to cover the peas by 5 cm. Bring to the boil, then reduce the heat to medium and cook for 5 minutes. Skim off any scum that forms on the surface using a spoon. Add the bay leaf and garlic cloves and simmer for 40 minutes. Add the salt and simmer for 20 more minutes until the peas are soft. Drain any excess liquid and remove the bay leaf. Purée with the olive oil and vinegar until very smooth.

TO SERVE: *This Greek-inspired purée is lovely with flash-fried capers over the top and as a side to grilled lamb skewers or simple grilled fish or squid. It's also lovely as a dip with crudités and a bowl of olives.*

BROCCOLI STEAKS WITH CHIMICHURRI AND BRAZIL NUTS

Serves 4

Being in the great parrillas of Buenos Aires and not being able to face meat can be a cruel curse. Yet that's what can happen when your adventures in South America coincide with the full throes of morning/ all-day sickness. There were many nights when I was caught between a rock of bleeding-rare steaks and the hard place of stodgy pastas when I wished this broccoli dish was on offer. By cleaving a head of broccoli into 'steaks' and charring it on a grill you not only have some visual novelty (it closely resembles the transverse of a tree), but it brings out the brassica's inherent meaty and nutty taste. The accompanying chimichurri is a trilling South American sauce traditionally served with steaks; it's a busy slurry of herbs, heat and here, the vibrancy of orange. Serve it over the broccoli, but also don't be shy about sloshing it over a piece of red meat or two. These days I like a rump steak, medium-rare.

1–2 heads of broccoli/600 g, stems trimmed 3 cm below the florets and remaining head of broccoli cleaved vertically into 4 'steaks' approximately 2 cm thick
2 tbsp olive oil
1 tsp dried chilli flakes
35 g Brazil nuts, roughly chopped
sea salt

Chimichurri
handful of picked fresh flat-leaf parsley leaves
handful of picked fresh oregano leaves
handful of picked fresh coriander leaves
1 tbsp finely chopped coriander stems
½ garlic clove, peeled
60 ml good-quality olive oil
grated zest of ½ orange
2 tbsp orange juice
1 tsp red wine vinegar
fresh chilli, to taste

To make the chimichurri, put the fresh herbs, garlic and olive oil in a blender or food processor. Whizz until smooth. Add the orange zest and juice, and the vinegar. Briefly blend to combine.

Add salt and chilli to taste (I wouldn't be shy about either of them). If you think it can handle more garlic, grate a little more in, but be careful – the flavour will become stronger over time.

To cook the broccoli, preheat a barbecue/grill pan to medium–high. Brush each 'steak' with the olive oil, sprinkle with the chilli flakes and season with salt. Barbecue with the hood down over the barbecue, or griddle with a metal bowl covering the steaks until lightly charred and cooked through – about 5–6 minutes per side. Serve the charred broccoli drizzled with chimichurri and sprinkled with the Brazil nuts, for crunch.

SAVOURY BAKED APPLES WITH GOATS' CURD AND PARMA HAM

Serves 6

Baked apples, stuffed with butter, cinnamon, walnuts, currants and almonds were a favourite pudding of my late English grandmother. She served them warm with cold custard, the outsides of the apples as wrinkled as the backs of her hands. Here I've taken them on a savoury route. They provide a lovely companion for a bitter green salad, perhaps with roast chicken as a centrepiece. You can use most red apples, which have a good crunch and bite. Green may prove a little too tart. You could also substitute the goats' curd mix for skinned sausagemeat for a heartier twist, or swap the goats' curd for blue cheese if you want something richer. The lavender, while not essential at all, does add a subtle floral note to the goats' curd, which in turn picks up some of the country-lane-sweetness in a Royal Gala apple.

6 small red eating apples (I like Royal Gala)
8 slices (80 g) of Parma ham, 6 cut in half lengthways,
  2 cut into thirds to create large postage-stamp squares
30 g hazelnuts, toasted and roughly chopped
30 g almonds, toasted and roughly chopped
170 g goats' curd
1 tbsp finely chopped fresh rosemary leaves
a pinch of unsprayed lavender leaves (optional)
a drizzle of olive oil
200 ml apple cider or apple juice
sea salt and freshly ground black pepper
a handful of salad leaves per person

Equipment
apple corer or melon baller

Preheat the oven to 150°C/300°F/Gas 2.

Cut the tops off the apples, about 1 cm below the stalk, then set the tops aside. Use an apple corer or a melon baller to remove the core of the apple and fashion a tunnel about as thick as a wine cork through the centre. You want the walls of the remaining apple to be 1–1.5 cm thick. Discard the cores. Using a sharp knife, score a shallow slit around the perimeter of each apple, about 1 cm below the top (this will help the apples not to burst during baking).

Take one postage-stamp square of ham and shimmy it down to the bottom of the tunnel and let the corners snake up the sides – you want to create a 'plug' for the filling so it doesn't fall out the bottom during baking.

Combine the chopped nuts with the goats' curd, rosemary and lavender, if you fancy. Add the olive oil and mash with a fork to combine.

Divide the filling into 6 and press each portion into the hollow in each apple, being careful not to push out the ham plug at the bottom.

Wrap 2 sheets of Parma ham around each apple. Use the fattiest parts of ham as glue to help it stick to the fruit. If it really won't stick, you can always use a cocktail stick to fasten it in place.

Put the apples in a baking dish and drizzle the tops with a little olive oil. Pour the cider or apple juice into the baking dish and place the tops of the apples in there too.

Cover the tray with foil (try not to let the foil touch the filling) and bake in the preheated oven for 40 minutes. Remove the foil, turn the oven temperature up to 180°C/350°F/Gas 4 and bake for another 20 minutes or until the apples are soft and the ham is crisp.

Serve the apples warm, with the tops at a jaunty angle for presentation, with salad leaves and a drizzling of the cooking juices from the bottom of the dish.

BRUSSELS SPROUTS WITH HAZELNUTS, LENTILS AND MUSTARD DRESSING

Serves 4

I finally got my taste of Buenos Aires in Sydney of all places. Porteño in Surry Hills is the parrilla you dreamed of finding in San Telmo, but never quite happened upon. Besides the whole beasts that loll over a wood-burning fire, what they're famed for are their Brussels sprouts, which are deep fried, and magical. This is a slightly lighter version using the heat of the oven, with some chew and sweetness coming from pairing them with dried apple and hazelnuts.
I like to eat them with some grilled lamb or beef, but for a vegetarian twist, try them with the Broccoli Steaks with Chimichurri and Brazil Nuts on page 68. Tango tunes in the background are entirely optional.

500 g Brussels sprouts, bases trimmed, and cut in half
4 tbsp olive oil
a generous pinch of sea salt
70 g hazelnuts, roughly chopped (in half is fine)
2 tbsp finely chopped dried apple (optional)
handful of fresh flat-leaf parsley, roughly chopped

Dressed lentils
50 g small French green lentils, eg Puy lentils
50 ml extra virgin olive oil
25 ml apple cider vinegar
2 tbsp brown sugar
1–2 tsp hot English mustard (or Dijon if you prefer
  a milder flavour)

Preheat the oven to 200°C/400°F/Gas 6.

Place the Brussels sprouts, cut side up, snugly in a baking dish. Drizzle with the olive oil and season with the salt. Scatter the hazelnuts around the sprouts. Bake them in the preheated oven for 40 minutes, or until the tops are bronzed and the centres are soft.

While the sprouts are roasting, make the dressed lentils. Rinse the lentils well and place them in a saucepan with enough cold water to cover them by 2 cm. Bring the water to the boil and cook the lentils for 15–20 minutes, until just tender.

Whisk together the oil, vinegar, brown sugar and mustard in a small saucepan over low heat until it barely simmers. You want it to be both emulsified and warmed through. Taste it. If you like a stronger mustard flavour, add another teaspoon and whisk it well to combine.

Drain the cooked lentils, add them to the warm dressing and toss to combine. If you fancy the dried apple, add it now as well.

Scatter the dressed lentils over the top of the roasted sprouts and hazelnuts. Top with the parsley.

TIP: *If you were pressed for time you could easily substitute the Puy lentils for a tin of lentils, rinsed, well drained and then combined with the warm dressing in a saucepan to gently heat them through.*

CAULIFLOWER AND BROCCOLI GRATIN

Serves 4

A cauliflower or broccoli 'cheese' was my definition of childhood comfort – probably because one of the first things my mother taught me to make was béchamel. I remember sitting on the kitchen bench and watching her methodically stirring the warmed milk into the roux, coaxing it into a silky consistency. It would then be poured over broccoli and cauliflower florets and baked until the top puckered and blistered. This dish goes a slightly different route and has a sneaky substitution of a cheese-gilded cauliflower purée as the sauce. Look, mum! No flour! You'd be hard pressed to taste the difference. Instead, it's a concentrated combination of soft and crisp vegetables, a little dairy and still plenty of satisfying squish. It's comfort food at its best (and is lovely with chicken, steak, or good-quality sausages).

400 g cauliflower, green bits discarded, cut into small florets
  and stem diced
200 ml water
100 g mozzarella or provolone cheese, grated
1 large head of broccoli (650 g), cut into florets
30 g Parmesan, grated
25 g flaked almonds
a pinch of dried chilli flakes (optional)
sea salt

Put the cauliflower and water in a saucepan, cover with the lid and simmer over medium heat for 15 minutes, stirring occasionally to prevent it catching or scorching. Remove the lid and simmer for another 10 minutes, or until the cauliflower is soft, stirring occasionally. Season with a pinch of salt, then use a stick blender or food processor to blend the cauliflower to a smooth cream.

Return the cauliflower purée to the saucepan and add the mozzarella or provolone. Stir over low heat until the cheese has melted through.

Preheat a grill to high.

Steam the broccoli for 3 minutes or until al dente.

Transfer the broccoli to a baking dish and pour the cheesy cauliflower sauce over it. Sprinkle the top with the Parmesan and flaked almonds. Place under the grill for 7 minutes or until the top has bronzed and the almonds have browned. Add chilli flakes if you want an extra kick, and serve hot.

CHICKPEAS, LEEK, APPLE AND PEAR SALAD

Serves 2

This is a warming autumnal tangle, with the sweetness of the leeks amplified by slivers of dried pear and crisp apple. The simple process of introducing the fennel seeds and garlic to the olive oil over medium heat helps them to infuse and creates a lovely base for a dressing. While the chickpeas add some structure, you could easily substitute them for white beans or steamed segments of cauliflower. I often find myself serving this as a side dish to the Blue Cheese Soufflés (page 120) on a Sunday night when the air is starting to nip, following it up with a portion of the Rhubarb, Apple and Berry Slow Crumble (page 167).

1 tbsp fennel seeds
4 tbsp olive oil
2 garlic cloves, peeled and thinly sliced
1 leek, cut in half lengthways, rinsed and sliced 3 mm thick
1 x 400-g tin of chickpeas, rinsed
3 tbsp dried pear, finely sliced
1 tbsp apple cider vinegar
2 tbsp almonds, toasted and roughly chopped
½ Pink Lady apple, cut into very thin slivers
sea salt and freshly ground black pepper

Place a frying pan over medium heat, add the fennel seeds and toast for 1 minute.

Add half the olive oil and the garlic. Turn down the heat and sauté for 2 minutes, being careful not to scorch the garlic. Add the leek and cook for 8–10 minutes until soft, then add the chickpeas to warm through.

Toss the contents of the pan with the dried pear. Season with salt and pepper and dress with the remaining olive oil and the vinegar. Top with the toasted almonds and slivers of apple.

'THREE BEANS' WITH BASIL PESTO

Serves 4

Green beans with pesto is a classic combination in Liguria, where it's often paired with a double white-starch hit of pasta and potato. If you're after something a little lighter, try this version of a three-bean salad. There's still the textural crunch of the green beans against a slick basil sauce, but the inclusion of borlotti and white beans make for a more sustaining energy boost (you could also substitute the borlotti beans for black beans). Serve this either warm or cold, as part of an antipasto platter with roasted tomatoes, olives and aubergine, or as a simple side dish to grilled chicken or roast lamb.

90 g fresh basil leaves
45 g pine nuts, toasted
125 ml extra virgin olive oil
45 g Parmesan, finely grated
2 garlic cloves, peeled and grated
juice of ½ lemon
1 x 400-g tin of borlotti or black beans, rinsed
1 x 400-g tin of cannellini or other white beans, rinsed
300 g green beans, topped and tailed and cut into thirds
2 tbsp pumpkin seeds
sea salt and freshly ground black pepper

Make a pesto by pounding the basil, pine nuts, olive oil, Parmesan, garlic and lemon juice together either with a pestle and mortar, or blitzing them to a paste in a food processor. Check the seasoning and adjust to taste.

Place all 3 sets of beans in a saucepan and warm them with the pesto over low heat until the green beans are cooked but still retain some bite. Don't cook for too long, as the pesto may turn an unsightly shade of brown.

Serve the salad warm with the pumpkin seeds scattered over the top.

CAULIFLOWER 'COUSCOUS' WITH ALMONDS, CURRANTS AND MINT

Serves 4–6

This is a nifty trick. It turns out that by grating a cauliflower or giving it a swift tumble in a food processor, you can transform its rubbly nodules into small grains that closely resemble couscous. You can serve it raw, but I find a few minutes in a frying pan help to coax the best flavour out of them. From there, the rest is pure instinct. This salad takes its cue from my favourite way to consume couscous. The currants are plumped up by the bergamot tannins in Earl Grey tea and the almonds and herbs provide the necessary colour and texture. You can try serving this under a tagine (perhaps the Lamb Shank and Fig Tagine on page 128) or on its own with a tahini-yoghurt dressing and some barbecued chicken, fish or lamb. Incidentally, the tahini-yoghurt dressing also makes an excellent marinade for chicken or lamb. Try making double and leaving the proteins to marinate in the fridge for 30 minutes before baking or grilling them.

75 g currants
125 ml strong, hot Earl Grey tea
2 tbsp olive oil
1 large head of cauliflower, grated on a box grater into small fragments like chubby couscous grains (1 head should provide approximately 4 cups)
a pinch of sea salt
grated zest and juice of ½ lemon
40 g flaked almonds, toasted and chopped
small bunch of fresh flat-leaf parsley, chopped
small bunch of fresh mint, chopped

Tahini-yoghurt dressing
1 tbsp tahini
150 g Greek yoghurt
1 tbsp olive oil
grated zest and juice of ½ lemon

Soak the currants in the Earl Grey tea for 10–15 minutes until they have plumped up.

In the meantime, place a large frying pan over medium heat and add the olive oil, cauliflower grains and salt. Sauté for 5 minutes to help remove the raw taste from the cauliflower.

Transfer the contents of the pan to a bowl with the lemon zest and juice, almonds, fresh herbs and plumped, drained currants. Stir to combine.

To make the tahini-yoghurt dressing, mix all the ingredients together to combine.

Serve the 'couscous' with the tahini-yoghurt dressing on the side, or underneath a tagine.

DAL

Serves 2 as a main or 4 as a side

A great dal recipe is an asset for life. A note: while yellow split peas and chana dal look very similar, they are different (if you look closely, dal have a rippled exterior). It's the yellow split peas which cook down to mush more quickly, whereas the hardier dal will allow you to take a hand whisk to them after cooking, providing a good textural mix of rough and smooth. In order to insert a good jolt of flavour, cook the tarka seasoning separately and then fold it through at the end. The apple cider vinegar is not a traditional inclusion, but I think you'll find it does wonders.

225 g chana dal, soaked in 500 ml water for 1 hour
800 ml water
1 tsp ground turmeric

Tarka seasoning
1 onion, peeled
3 Roma tomatoes
2 garlic cloves, peeled
2 tbsp neutral-tasting oil
1 tbsp ground cumin
1 tsp ground turmeric
1 tsp ground coriander
½ tsp ground cinnamon
1 tsp ground ginger
1 tsp sea salt
1 tbsp apple cider vinegar

To serve
fresh coriander and chopped red chilli

Drain the soaked dal and rinse it well until the water runs clear.

Put the dal in a heavy-based saucepan or casserole dish with the water and turmeric. Set over medium heat and bring to the boil, skimming off any froth that forms on the surface using a spoon. Lower the heat so that the water is just simmering and clamp on a lid. Cook for about 40 minutes, checking occasionally to make sure there is still enough liquid in the pan. When the dal is pliable and there's a scant amount of liquid left, take the pan off the heat. (If the dal is soft but you still have an excess of water, drain off all but about 100 ml of the cooking liquid.) Use a whisk to form a rough purée out of the dal and liquid.

To make the tarka seasoning, use a food processor to blitz the onion, tomatoes and garlic to a paste.

Heat the oil in a frying pan and fry all the spices for 1–2 minutes, until fragrant. Add the onion-tomato paste and cook over medium heat for 2–3 minutes until everything has darkened and the raw onion taste has disappeared.

Stir the tarka seasoning, salt and vinegar into the dal and heat through before serving with coriander and chilli sprinkled over the top.

SMOKEY AUBERGINE WITH TOMATOES, PICKLED ONION, PARSLEY AND POMEGRANATE MOLASSES

Serves 4

This dish transports me straight to Zübeyir Ocakbaşi, a historic terrace in Istanbul, on a side street near the main shopping boulevard of Istiklal Caddesi. You can smell the restaurant before you see it, as most of the food is grilled over coals in the centre of the downstairs dining room. This side is a slightly more refined version of their 'Special Aubergine Salad'. Here it's accented with the crunch of walnuts and sweetness of softened onions. Over time I've discovered the best way to get the soft texture and smokey aroma in the aubergine is to place it whole, directly over a gas burner, occasionally turning it until the skin is withered and the insides are as pulpy as an over ripe piece of fruit. I like to eat this with simple charred meat or offal (in Istanbul we had skewers of liver, which were sublime) and perhaps the Cauliflower 'Couscous' with Almonds, Currants and Mint (page 76) as part of a wider mezze or barbecue feast for a group.

1 red onion, peeled and cut into half-moons,
  as slim as you can manage
1 tsp sea salt
2 tbsp red wine vinegar
2 large aubergines
2 tbsp olive oil
5-cm lump of ginger root, peeled and grated
1 brown onion, peeled and cut into slim half-moons
2 tbsp pomegranate molasses
2 tbsp water
2 Roma tomatoes, diced
small handful of fresh flat-leaf parsley, chopped
50 g walnuts, roughly chopped
sea salt and freshly ground black pepper

To serve
labneh, feta, soft eggs or grilled lamb (optional)

Place half of the red onion in a bowl with the salt and vinegar. Leave the onion to steep for 15–30 minutes until it has begun to turn translucent and the raw taste has softened.

Using tongs or similar, carefully hold an aubergine directly over a gas burner. Allow it to char for 5 minutes on each side, until the skin is black and puckered and the insides feel pulpy and soft. Transfer it to a bowl and cover the bowl with clingfilm. Repeat the with the other aubergine and add it to the bowl, too.

Leave the charred aubergines to sit and steam under the clingfilm for 10–15 minutes while you get started on the rest of the sauce.

Heat the olive oil in a frying pan or wok and add the ginger, brown onion and the remaining, raw red onion. Sauté over medium heat for 10 minutes, or until the onions have softened. Add the pomegranate molasses and water and sauté for another 5–10 minutes until you have a soft, pliable tangle of onions.

Remove the aubergines from the bowl, peel off the charred skins and discard them. Roughly chop the softened, smoked flesh and combine it with the onions in the pan to warm it through. Taste and season with salt and pepper if needed.

Top the warm mixture with the tomatoes, pickled and drained red onion, parsley and walnuts. Serve either warm or at room temperature, with labneh, feta, soft eggs or grilled lamb, if you like.

ROAST BEETROOT AND CARROTS WITH RAS EL HANOUT, MINT AND LABNEH

Serves 2 (or 4 if paired with the recipe to the right, here)

Beetroot and carrots may skirt a little higher in the GI stakes than some vegetables, but this sweet and jewelled combination of them with the freshness of mint and labneh, is just too good to miss – particularly when coupled with a ras el hanout spice blend (which translates as 'top of the shop' and may include up to 30 aromatics). The smell of it all transports me straight back to the souks of Marrakech. I like to treat this dish as an adornment to a meal, perhaps serving it with a sustaining base of the yellow split peas (to the right) and some chicken or lamb kebabs from the barbecue.

4 medium carrots (about 450 g), peeled
1 tbsp orange marmalade
4 tbsp olive oil
8 small cooked baby beetroot (150 g), drained
  (from a tin or packet will suffice)
2 tsp sea salt flakes
2 tbsp ras el hanout
20 g flaked almonds, toasted
2 tbsp labneh (strained Greek yoghurt) or goats' feta,
  crumbled
20 fresh mint leaves, torn

Preheat the oven to 200°C/400°F/Gas 6.

Cut 3½ of the carrots into batons. Set the remaining half-carrot aside.

In a small saucepan, combine the marmalade and olive oil. Warm it gently and whisk it to emulsify.

Combine the carrot batons and beetroot in a roasting dish with the marmalade mixture and sprinkle with the salt and ras el hanout. Roast in the preheated oven for 50 minutes or until the vegetables have taken on a burnished hue and are cooked through.

Shave the remaining half-carrot into ribbons using a vegetable peeler.

Serve the roasted vegetables with the almonds, labneh, carrot ribbons and mint leaves scattered over the top.

YELLOW SPLIT PEAS WITH BURNT BUTTER AND ORANGE

Serves 4

This dish is the taste of sunshine. There's warmth from the ginger and chilli and some exuberance from the orange. By simply drizzling the pulses with a nut-brown butter that's primped with garlic and toasted almonds, somehow it elevates a slick of yellow peas into something stunning. When I'm not serving this dish alongside the Roast Beetroot and Carrots with Ras el Hanout, Mint and Labneh (opposite) and some protein, fresh from the barbecue, I like to eat it as is, topped with a five-minute egg so the orange yolk can slowly seep into the base, blurring orange into yellow, creating a molten tumble of warmth.

1 tbsp olive oil
1 red onion, peeled, halved and cut into thin slivers
5-cm lump of ginger root, peeled
2 red chillies, 1 halved, 1 finely diced
½ orange
200 g yellow split peas, rinsed
400 ml hot water

Burnt butter
1 tsp olive oil
2 garlic cloves, peeled and thinly sliced
2 tbsp butter
2 tbsp almonds, roughly chopped into thirds

To serve
2 tbsp plain yoghurt, and chia seeds (optional)

Heat the olive oil in a heavy-based saucepan or casserole dish over medium heat. Add the onion, ginger, the halved chilli and the orange, cut side down, and sauté for 7–10 minutes until the onion has softened and the orange is starting to gain some colour. Add the split peas and hot water and bring to the boil. Cover the pan with the lid and simmer for 45 minutes, or until the liquid has largely been absorbed and the split peas have cooked but not completely broken down. (If there is an excess of liquid and the peas have cooked, drain some of the liquid.) Squeeze any remaining juice from the orange into the pan, then remove it and the lump of ginger.

For the burnt butter, put the olive oil, garlic, diced chilli, butter and almonds into a frying pan over medium heat. Heat until the butter has turned nut-brown.

Serve the split peas with a drizzle of yoghurt and the burnt butter. Sprinkle over some chia seeds if you fancy.

BLACK BEAN, CHORIZO, SWEET POTATO AND COCONUT BOWL

Serves 2

Out of all of the pulses that play hide and seek in tins at the back of your kitchen cupboard, black beans may be my favourite. To liven up this chunky salad I add red onion in two textures – softly roasted and thinly sliced and raw. There's a tiny touch of chorizo for richness (though if you wanted to skip the pork and fat, smoked paprika sprinkled over the sweet potato would also work nicely). And then there are some green herbs and yoghurt to link it all together. It's lovely piping hot and just as good at room temperature. Here are some more good things about it: you can happily eat it out of a bowl with a fork; you could easily add some chicken, prawns or squid for extra protein; and at the very end you'll only find one pan to wash up. Like all warm salads like this, the quantities and combinations of flavours are a little fluid. If you don't have sweet potato, but have pumpkin, substitute it. If you hate coriander, then swap it for mint. If you can't find coconut shavings then flaked almonds would also work well.

1 large sweet potato, peeled and cubed
2 tbsp olive oil
50 g chorizo, cut into thin coins and then in half (if vegetarian, omit this and sprinkle the sweet potato with 1 tsp ground cumin and 1 tsp smoked paprika)
handful of dried coconut shavings
1 red onion, peeled and cut into eighths
1 x 400-g tin of black beans, rinsed
handful of fresh coriander (or mint if you hate coriander)
1 red chilli, thinly sliced
Greek yoghurt, to drizzle (optional)
sea salt and freshly ground black pepper

Preheat the oven to 180°C/350°F/Gas 4.

Place the sweet potato in a roasting tray, drizzle with the olive oil and season with salt. Roast it in the preheated oven for 20 minutes or until it's gained a little colour around the edges.

After 20 minutes, add the chorizo, coconut shavings and most of the onion (leave one-eighth aside to sliver raw at the end). Roast for 20 minutes.

When the potato is cooked through and the onion has been stained slightly pink from the chorizo's oil, remove the tray from the oven and mix in the black beans. The heat from the roasting tray and its contents will help warm the beans.

Cut the remaining onion pieces into slivers as thin you can manage. Add the onion slivers, coriander and chilli to the roasting tray.

Season with salt and pepper and drizzle Greek yoghurt over the top before serving.

KALE CAESAR

Serves 4–6

There's more to this salad than the punning novelty of its name (though it is also something to hail). It takes that 90s cafe favourite and updates it with crispy chickpeas standing in for croutons, and raw, fine ribbons of kale for cos. If you're searching for a little more substance, add in some soft egg or grilled chicken (since we've tinkered with everything else, this is hardly the time to get snippy about whether chicken has any place in a true Caesar salad). If you're not up to eating raw egg yolks (pregnant, immune compromised etc), then you can always whizz the capers, anchovies and lemon zest through shop-bought whole-egg mayonnaise and thin it with lemon juice until you get the right consistency.

3 rashers of bacon, cut into thin batons
1 x 400-g tin of chickpeas, rinsed
1 tbsp olive oil
400 g kale, hard stems discarded and leaves shredded
    into ribbons 5 mm wide
40 g Parmesan, shaved

Dressing
1 egg yolk
2 tsp Dijon mustard
1 garlic clove, peeled
2 tsp capers, drained
2 marinated anchovy fillets in oil, drained
175 ml sunflower oil
grated zest and juice of 1 lemon
sea salt and freshly ground black pepper

To serve
2 hard-boiled eggs, or cooked or grilled chicken (optional)

Preheat the oven to 220°C/425°F/Gas 7.

Put the bacon and chickpeas on a baking tray and drizzle with the olive oil. Bake in the preheated oven for 20 minutes, or until the bacon is very crisp and the chickpeas have developed a brittle crust.

To make the dressing, combine the egg yolk, mustard, garlic clove, capers and anchovies in a blender and blend until smooth. Slowly drip in the oil, drop by drop, to make a dressing. Then drizzle in the lemon juice and whizz for a few seconds to combine. Season with salt and pepper.

Combine the kale with the lemon zest and the dressing. Top with the crispy bacon and chickpeas, and the Parmesan shavings.

If you fancy a little more protein, grate or break the hard-boiled eggs over the top of the salad, or mix through some shredded cooked chicken.

GADO GADO INDONESIAN VEGETABLE SALAD WITH SPICY PEANUT SAUCE

Serves 2

I should say upfront that this version of the classic Indonesian vegetable salad topped with satay sauce is much closer to what I made when I was studying Bahasa as a 13-year-old in Sydney than what you'd find in a kantin in Jakarta. But at its heart what remains is a great way to gussy up greens and the like when you just can't face one more stir-fry. You can substitute whichever vegetables you prefer: carrot batons and courgette would make fine additions. The traditional iteration will have a more exotic blend of roots and spices. It will also commonly play host to hard-boiled eggs. On a Wednesday night I prefer this quick version. I also like how the runny yolk in a five-minute egg adds a golden gloss to the dressing. Serve this on its own, or as a more substantial side for grilled chicken or fish.

100 g mangetout, cut into thirds
100 g broccoli or broccolini, cut into manageable pieces
1 red pepper, deseeded and cut into batons
¼ white cabbage, finely shredded
50 g beansprouts
2 eggs, boiled for 5 minutes, then plunged into cold water and shelled

Spicy peanut sauce
3 tbsp peanut butter (crunchy or smooth)
2 tbsp cashews
grated zest and juice of 1 lime
2-cm lump of ginger root, peeled and grated
1 garlic clove, peeled and grated
1 small red chilli, deseeded and chopped
3 tbsp water
1½ tsp light soy sauce
a pinch of sugar

Lightly steam the mangetout and broccoli or broccolini until they are soft but still retain some bite. Combine the steamed vegetables with the raw red pepper, cabbage and beansprouts and divide between 2 plates.

To make the spicy peanut sauce, put all the ingredients in a food processor and whizz to a paste.

Dab the plates of salad with the sauce. Place the peeled, boiled egg in the centre of the plate and allow people to puncture their own yolk.

BORLOTTI BEANS WITH ROASTED PEAR, WALNUTS AND BLUE CHEESE

Serves 2

To me, borlotti beans are the strong, silent member of the pulse clan. Faintly brown and meekly nutty, they need to marry with some stronger flavours before they really begin to shine. This simple tray bake calls on the flavours you'd find on a good cheese board and throws them together. Red onion and burnished pear provide plump sweetness. There's the crumble of toasted almonds. And then there are small nuggets of blue cheese. I prefer Saint Agur, a not too assertive blue from the Auvergne region of France, though feel free to experiment with whichever type you prefer. This is a dish that pairs nicely with cooked chicken thighs as a warm salad, or if you're feeling jolly, double or triple it and serve it alongside a roast turkey.

2 tbsp extra virgin olive oil
1 x 400-g tin of borlotti beans, rinsed
1 red onion, peeled and cut into eighths
handful of walnuts
2 medium pears, cored and cut into eighths
2 handfuls of green leaves (eg rocket, baby spinach, watercress)
40 g blue cheese (I like Saint Agur)
juice of ½ lemon

Preheat the oven to 160°C/325°F/Gas 3.

Drizzle half the olive oil into a baking dish and scatter the borlotti beans over it.

Top with the onion, walnuts and three-quarters of the pear wedges. Drizzle with the remaining olive oil.

Bake in the preheated oven for about 1 hour, or until the onion pieces are soft, the walnuts toasted and the pear softened.

Combine all the contents of the baking dish with the green leaves. Shave the remaining pieces of pear into ribbons using a vegetable peeler and scatter over the top. Crumble in the blue cheese and dress with a little lemon juice just before serving.

This is bright food, designed for long days and languid nights. It's the sort of supper you don't mind making when you know that there's a good chance tomorrow will involve either a bathing suit or a pair of shorts. In these pages are the sorts of feasts which take me on holiday even if I'm tethered to the kitchen. As soon as I'm sitting down to a plate of Thai green papaya salad, piri piri chicken or Moroccan lamb and chickpea burgers, I'm elsewhere. And on the nights when The Hungry One and I are standing watch by the barbecue, supervising the production of griddled chillies stuffed with feta and black beans, or tandoori salmon with spiced lentils, we're never happier to be home.

LEAN

SUMMER

FEASTS

SEABASS SWADDLED IN COURGETTE RIBBONS

Serves 2

Those with a plot will understand the plight: what do you do with the end-of-season glut of courgettes? Once, you might have snuck them into cakes or breads. Certainly, you can sauté slices by the stack, or practise your pickles. But might I suggest you put them to work here? Swaddling a skinless fillet of fish in overlapping strips of green and white calls for just a few minutes of craft with a vegetable peeler, but leaves a lasting visual impression. One other bonus is how it protects the delicate flesh of white fish fillets from the heat of a grill or a pan. I find it's worth getting a good char on the crust to contrast with the pliant 'noodle salad' on the side, which is made from the remaining ribbons of courgette and glossed with a perky salsa verde. Additionally, ribbons of courgette make an excellent substitution for noodles in many dishes – try them wafting in chicken or miso soup, or dressed with pesto for a lighter version of pasta.

2–3 medium courgettes
2 fillets of skinless seabass or other white-fleshed fish, about 100 g each
1 lemon, halved
1 tbsp olive oil
handful of flaked almonds, toasted
sea salt

Parsley and tarragon salsa verde
small handful of fresh tarragon leaves
large handful of fresh flat-leaf parsley leaves
60 ml olive oil
½ garlic clove, peeled and grated
2 marinated anchovy fillets in oil, drained
1 tsp capers, drained
juice of ½ lemon

Using a vegetable peeler or mandolin, shred the courgettes lengthways into ribbons.

Pat the fish fillets dry with kitchen paper. Take a piece of baking paper and lay out 12 overlapping ribbons of courgette side by side on the paper. Place a fish fillet horizontally across the courgette ribbons and use the paper to help swaddle the fillet in the ribbons. Turn the fish seam side down. Repeat with 12 more ribbons and the second fish fillet. Place the fillets in the fridge until you are ready to cook them.

To make the parsley and tarragon salsa verde, whizz all the ingredients together in a food processor. Taste and season with salt and whizz again until you have a zippy slurry you are happy with.

Combine the remaining courgette ribbons with the salsa verde and divide between 2 plates.

To cook the fish, place a large frying pan over medium–high heat. You can test if the pan's surface is hot enough by placing the lemon halves, cut side down, in the pan. When it is ready, they should sizzle. Drizzle the olive oil in the hot pan, then add the fish fillets, seam side down. Cook them for 3–5 minutes, until the ribbons have taken on some char. Gently flip them over, trying not to unravel the ribbons, and cook them for 2 minutes on the other side until the fish has cooked through.

Serve the grilled fish with the burnished lemon halves, dressed courgette ribbons and flaked almonds. If you need something else on the side, some steamed green beans, White Bean Purée (page 67), Fennel Purée (page 66) or Cauliflower Purée (page 66) would do nicely.

VITELLO TONNATO WITH GREEN BEAN AND TOMATO SALAD

Serves 6

This dish is protein, squared. It translates as slices of lean veal, seasoned with a sauce made from tuna. Before you turn the page in disbelief, bear with me. This is a classic Piedmontese combination, often served as part of an antipasto platter. Here it's repurposed as a main course that's perfect for a small group. Just sear the nut of veal, then leave it in the oven or on the barbecue to roast while you make the sauce and assemble the salad. What you get in the end is a canny combination; somehow the mellow meat finds new life with the briney acidity of the tuna sauce.

1.8 kg nut of veal (a boneless cut from the leg)
   at room temperature
2 tsp sea salt
1 tsp freshly ground black pepper
2 tbsp olive oil

Tuna sauce
2 egg yolks
1 tsp Dijon mustard
150 ml neutral-tasting oil
1 tbsp capers, drained
2 marinated anchovy fillets in oil, drained
185 g tinned tuna in olive oil
juice of ½ lemon

Salad
300 g green beans, steamed
4 tomatoes, sliced
1 red onion, peeled and cut into slivers
1 small bunch of fresh basil
2 tbsp olive oil
1 tsp red wine vinegar

To serve
2 tbsp capers, patted dry and fried in 2 tbsp olive oil until
   they open up like flowers

Preheat a barbecue with a hood, or your oven to 160°C/325°F/Gas 3.

Season the veal with the salt and pepper. Drizzle the oil into either the flat plate of a barbecue or a frying pan over medium heat and sear the meat for 2 minutes on each side to form a nice brown crust.

Transfer the meat to a baking dish and place it in the preheated oven or simply pull down the hood of the barbecue to roast. Cook it for 1 hour and 15 minutes, or until the internal temperature is 55–60°C/130–140°F. Allow the meat to rest somewhere warm and under foil for 20–30 minutes before carving. The meat will continue to cook through as it rests. The ends will be more done and the centre pink.

To make the tuna sauce, put the egg yolks and mustard in a food processor and whizz to combine. With the motor running, slowly trickle in the oil, drop by drop, to create a mayonnaise. Once it has emulsified to a mayonnaise, add the capers, anchovies, tuna and its marinating oil, and lemon juice, and blitz to combine.

To make the salad, combine all the ingredients together.

Slice the rested meat into pieces 1 cm thick and serve topped with the tuna sauce, fried capers and the salad. This can be served warm, or at room temperature as part of a family-style feast.

TIP: *You want your veal to be blushing in the centre, so it's best to give it plenty of time to rest before you carve it to prevent any wayward puddles of pink juice on your plate. The best thing to do is carve on a separate board to the one you'll serve from.*

THAI GREEN PAPAYA
SALAD WITH TROUT

Serves 4

The sight of a green papaya salad takes me to two places. In one, I'm sporting black cotton fisherman's trousers I was certain were a good purchase at the time. I have sunburn on my shoulders and I'm overlooking the turquoise waters of Kata Noi beach. In the second, I've been pregnant and bloated for 283 days, and am once again wearing those same trousers (this time it's a choice determined by ease, not misguided elegance). Yet there's no reason to reserve the tingling enzymes of green papaya for Phuket, or the very end of pregnancy (green papaya being an ingredient rumoured to help bring on labour). The brilliant thing about these slender strands of unripe fruit, muddled with Thai basil, chilli and your choice of protein (I like trout, but prawns, chicken and duck are also great) is how light you'll feel after you've eaten them. Which means there's really no reason, bar comfort, to be swathing myself in loose, low-slung cotton trousers, is there?

1 kg green papaya (or green mango)
400 g cooked trout or prawns, peeled (or poached, shredded chicken, or roasted, sliced duck)
70 g roasted peanuts, roughly chopped
6 spring onions, green bits shredded
400 g cherry tomatoes, halved
handful of fresh Thai basil leaves, torn

Dressing
1 large red chilli, finely diced
2 garlic cloves, peeled and grated
1½ tbsp palm sugar, grated or brown muscovado sugar
4 tbsp lime juice
4 tbsp fish sauce
1 tbsp toasted sesame oil
3 tsp rice wine vinegar

To make the dressing, combine all the ingredients together and stir them until the sugar has dissolved.

Peel the skin off the papaya carefully. Use the shredding attachment on a mandolin to grate it, or cut it into sections and place them through the shredder of a food processor. If using a mango, be sure to avoid the stone.

Combine the salad ingredients with the dressing, reserving some of the peanuts to sprinkle on top.

CHICKEN SAN CHOI BOW

Serves 4

To me san choi bow is often the opening salvo in a meal spun on a lazy susan, gluggy with rice and culminating in deep-fried ice dairy. Yet there are plenty of ways to conjure the allure of a night at the local Chinese without installing a rotating circle in the middle of your dining table – or falling down a white carb hole. For one, leave the fried noodles, rice and water chestnuts behind. Instead invite some slivered jicama/yam bean to the party. This bulbous root is often found in Asian supermarkets and has a similar texture to a water chestnut, but less bloating starch. From there you can pad out your lettuce parcels with shaved carrot, mince and the crunch of peanuts. And if you still feel the need for something white to spin on the table, take comfort in the fact you can always buy a rotating disc from IKEA.

1 large iceberg lettuce
2 tsp vegetable oil
5 spring onions thinly sliced
2 tbsp chopped fresh coriander stems
5-cm lump of ginger root, peeled and grated
700 g chicken mince (or turkey or pork)
2 tbsp light soy sauce
3 tbsp hoisin sauce
1 tbsp chilli oil
1 tsp toasted sesame oil
½ jicama/yam bean (about 250 g), peeled and sliced
  on a mandolin, or 2 large handfuls of beansprouts
1 carrot, peeled and grated
2 tbsp roughly chopped roasted peanuts
2 tbsp chopped fresh coriander leaves

Cut the base off the iceberg lettuce and submerge in cold water to separate out the leaves. Trim them with scissors, if necessary, to make open cups. Place them in a bowl or sink of cold water to stay crisp.

Place a wok over high heat and add the vegetable oil. Stir-fry the spring onions, coriander stems and ginger for 1 minute to soften them. Add the mince and cook for 4–6 minutes, until it takes on some colour. Add the soy sauce, hoisin sauce, chilli oil and sesame oil.

Fold the stir-fry through the grated jicama/yam bean and carrot. Serve in the lettuce cups, top with the peanuts and coriander leaves, and supply napkins to catch any drips.

PEPPERS STUFFED WITH CHIA, HUMMUS AND PINE NUTS

Serves 2

Stuffed peppers aren't always the most appealing dish. In fact anyone who has ever dabbled with vegetarianism will probably have tasted some unspeakable versions, many of which more closely resemble miniature paddling pools than supper. The key is finding things to pad the centre that won't leach excess liquid, leaving a soppy mess on your plate. Enter the chia seeds, which have a remarkable ability to absorb any surplus fluid. What follows is a pretty dish that's perfect for a summer mezze spread. Try coupling it with a very crisp green salad and some pickles if there are just two of you at the table, or combine it with the Smokey Aubergine with Tomatoes, Pickled Onion, Parsley and Pomegranate Molasses (page 79) and some Quinoa and Courgette Fritters with Strained Yoghurt (page 40) and Roasted and Fresh Tomato Skewers with Mint and Halloumi (page 40) for a crowd.

200 g hummus
40 g chia seeds
1 tbsp lemon juice
1 tsp ground cumin
½ tsp chilli powder
1 red pepper, cut in half through the stem and deseeded
2 tbsp pine nuts
2 tbsp olive oil

To serve
bitter leaves and chilli sauce

Preheat the oven to 180°C/350°F/Gas 4.

In a small bowl, mix together the hummus, chia seeds, lemon juice and spices.

Portion the mixture into the cavities of the peppers. Top with the pine nuts and drizzle with the olive oil.

Put the peppers on a baking tray and bake them in the preheated oven for 40 minutes, or until they have puckered around the edges and the pine nuts have lightly bronzed.

Serve the stuffed peppers on a bed of bitter leaves, with chilli sauce on the side.

BROAD BEAN, FENNEL, MINT, LEMON AND PARMESAN SALAD

Serves 2

This is the kind of dish I make when there are clouds lazily bobbing across a blue sky and it's warm enough to peg your trousers around your calves. It's a quick pull-together salad which also manages to look quite smart. Here are some other winning features: it takes just as much time to make as it does to soft-boil an egg. It's delicious with a sun-shiny yolk strewn over the top. It's also grand on its own as a side for barbecued chicken, prawns, and both pink and white fish.

What you've got is a restrained balance of flavours – the mild aniseed of the fennel mellowed in olive oil, the sweetness of broad beans (frozen are fine – we've all got better things to do than pod beans), the richness of Parmesan and a breath of fresh air from the mint and lemon.

If you haven't got a mandolin, I recommend using a vegetable peeler or the shaving attachment on your food processor to try and get the right sort of thickness in the fennel. Fat hunks just won't cut it here. If it's a big mouthful of aniseed you're after, you'd be better off munching some black liquorice for dessert.

1 fennel bulb, finely shaved on a mandolin, with wafty green fennel tops reserved
200 g fresh or frozen broad beans (often available in Asian supermarkets)
grated zest and juice of ½ lemon
handful of fresh mint, finely chopped
30 g Parmesan, shaved
3 tbsp olive oil
sea salt and freshly ground black pepper

Trim the bottom off the fennel. Put the mandolin on the slimmest setting you can get and carefully shave the fennel onto a plate.

If using frozen broad beans, gently steam them to defrost them.

Combine the fennel shavings, fennel tops and beans with the lemon zest, the mint and Parmesan. Season with salt and pepper.

Make a dressing by combining the olive oil and lemon juice, then drizzle it over the salad.

SORT-OF-WALDORF SALAD

Serves 2

The original version of this salad was first invented more than a century ago at the Waldorf Hotel. Celery, mayonnaise, apple and walnuts were the key elements. These days I say you can keep your celery and wrinkled nuts along with your finery and napery. Here I've gone for fresh chunks of fennel and the crunch of almonds. For a dressing there's a lush slick of basil aïoli, though some basil leaves blended into thick Greek yoghurt would suffice in a pinch. The only thing delicate here are some ribbons of mint, rolled up like a cigar and cut lengthways, so they unfurl across the top of a salad like streamers. This is the sort of dish best eaten with a glass of chilled wine and possibly a bathrobe; not in a five-star hotel, but on your balcony at home.

3 cooked and cool or warm chicken thighs, cut into chunks
   the size of a wine cork (you could also use the meat off a
   shop-bought barbecue chicken)
2 tbsp basil aïoli (ie 2 tsp good-quality shop-bought pesto
   mixed into 2 tbsp good-quality mayonnaise)
1 fennel bulb, cut into small chunks
1 small Granny Smith apple, cored and cut into small chunks
½ avocado, pitted and diced
3 tsp flaked almonds, toasted
12 fresh mint leaves
sea salt and freshly ground black pepper

Combine the chicken with the basil aïoli, and fennel and apple chunks.

Gently add the avocado and sprinkle the almonds over the top.

Stack the mint leaves on top of each other. Roll them into a cigar widthways and slice them thinly lengthways to create little ribbons.

Add the mint ribbons to the salad and season with salt and pepper.

TIP: *Add the avocado just before serving. You want it to be fresh slivers of jade, not a sad mush of brown.*

TUNA NIÇOISE FISHCAKES

Makes 8–10 fishcakes, or serves 4
(and leftovers freeze well)

The fishcakes of my memories are leaden pucks of leftover mashed potato and flaked fish, often served with a limpid salad as an afterthought. This version is not only lighter, but breezier. The potato is replaced with white beans, which not only offer extra protein, but a nutty taste. The other flavours borrow heavily from the Provençal landscape of a Niçoise salad. Anchovies, capers, olives and lemon all make cameos. I like to serve these fishcakes with a salad of green beans, olives and blushingly ripe tomatoes drizzled with olive oil. If you feel like being slavishly devoted to the place of inspiration and can't find some nautical stripes to eat your dinner in, a soft-cooked egg relaxing over the top will help complete the picture.

2 x 400-g tins of white beans, rinsed
2 marinated anchovy fillets in olive oil, drained
grated zest and juice of 1 lemon
2 x 185-g tins of solid-packed tuna, drained and flaked
1 egg, lightly beaten
1 tbsp capers, diced
10 black olives, pitted and finely chopped
1 tsp freshly ground black pepper
3 tbsp chickpea (besan or gram) flour

For dusting and frying
115 g chickpea (besan or gram) flour
sunflower or olive oil

To serve
a salad of steamed green beans, olives, chopped cherry
   tomatoes and fresh basil leaves
lemon wedges

Blitz the white beans, anchovies, lemon zest and juice together until smooth, using a stick blender or a food processor.

Add the tuna, beaten egg, capers, olives, pepper and the 3 tablespoons chickpea flour to the mixture and stir to combine. Cover it and refrigerate for 1 hour if you have time – this will help the fishcakes to hold their shape.

When the mixture is ready to come out of the fridge, preheat the oven to 150°C/300°F/Gas 2.

Pour the 115 g dusting flour onto a plate. Parcel out 3 tablespoons of the tuna mixture and shape between your hands to a disc about 8 cm across and 2 cm high. Pat it in the flour until it's evenly coated all over. Repeat to form more patties with the remaining tuna mixture.

Pour enough oil in a large frying pan to make a depth of 1–2 mm. Set it over medium heat and when the oil begins to shimmer, add the fishcakes in batches of 3 and fry them for 1–2 minutes on each side, or until crispy and golden. Keep the fishcakes hot in the oven while you fry the remaining batches.

Serve the fishcakes hot with a salad of green beans, olives, cherry tomatoes and basil, and lemon wedges to squeeze over.

GRIDDLED CHILLIES STUFFED WITH FETA, BLACK BEANS AND PUMPKIN SEEDS

Serves 2

The inspiration for this dish came initially from my step-brother, a terrific cook in his own right, who one night for family dinner delivered from the barbecue a platter of blackened chillies stuffed with feta. It was an experiment that worked. This marries his thinking with a cleaner version of the Tex Mex classic of chiles rellenos omitting the battered crust and swapping the often greasy meat stuffing for rumpled black beans. The end result is a lovely light lunch when served with some guacamole on the side, and if you're in the mood, a margarita or two.

2–3 long red, banana chillies, split lengthways, seeds and
  internal membranes scraped out
1 x 400-g tin of black beans, rinsed and mashed with a potato
  masher (it can be rustic)
100 g feta, crumbled
3 tbsp pumpkin seeds
handful of fresh coriander leaves, chopped

To serve
1 lime
hot sauce
Guacamole (page 26)

To use a barbecue, preheat it to medium. Alternatively, use a griddle pan on the stove.

Stuff the peppers with the mashed black beans, then the feta.

Transfer the stuffed peppers to the barbecue or to a griddle pan and grill on each side (being careful that the stuffing doesn't fall out) for 4 minutes, or until the peppers are charred and blistered and the black beans have warmed through.

Top the peppers with the pumpkin seeds and coriander. Serve with cheeks of lime, hot sauce and guacamole.

PRAWN, AVOCADO AND EDAMAME SALAD

Serves 2

To me there's something quite meditative about popping these edamame (soybeans) out of their shells. If for some reason you need a bit of extra focus in your day, feel free to buy packs of frozen pods and pluck out the required beans one by one. For those who are doing just fine, many Asian supermarkets will sell frozen packs of edamame already shelled, like peas. In this salad they're combined with avocado, cucumber, leaves, lime and sesame, in what is essentially a zen take on prawn cocktail.

200 g shelled edamame beans
2 handfuls of green leaves (a mix of baby spinach, watercress and rocket is nice)
12 cm cucumber, shaved into ribbons with a vegetable peeler
200 g peeled, cooked prawns (heads and digestive tracts removed)
1 lime (grated zest and juice of one half, and the other half cut into wedges)
1 tsp toasted sesame oil
1 tbsp neutral-tasting oil
½ avocado, sliced
1½ tsp black sesame seeds (or toasted white sesame seeds)

Combine the edamame beans, green leaves, shaved cucumber and prawns. Add the lime zest.

Combine the lime juice with the oils and whisk to combine. Toss the dressing over the salad, then top with the avocado pieces and sesame seeds. Serve with the extra wedges of lime.

TIP: *I find it's best to gently place the avocado on the plate just before serving, to prevent it turning into unsightly mulch when you dress the salad. If you can't find edamame, feel free to substitute green peas, or broad beans.*

TANDOORI SALMON WITH SPICED LENTILS AND RAITA

Serves 4

This combination has swiftly become a midweek staple for not only our family, but a few of the testers who helped out in the production of this book. Why? Because it's aromatic but not too onerous and it easily halves or doubles, depending on how many are sitting at your table. But I think it's mainly because eating these yellow-hued lentils and rosy pink salmon makes us feel good, and not just because of the links between turmeric and reduced rates of cancer and dementia. Here are some tips: if you have the time, try to marinate your salmon for 30 minutes to help bed down the flavours. I do this while I'm making the lentils and setting the table. And be sure to include the sides of raita, fresh tomato, and a cheek of lemon for squeezing – they really help to awaken the dish.

4 fillets of salmon (about 180 g each), skin on
1 tbsp olive oil
sea salt

Marinade
150 g Greek yoghurt
1 garlic clove, peeled and grated
2-cm lump of ginger root, peeled and grated
1 tsp ground cumin
1 tsp ground turmeric
a pinch of sea salt
½ tsp freshly ground black pepper
1 tsp paprika
½–1 tsp cayenne pepper

Spiced lentils
1 tbsp ground turmeric
1 tsp ground cumin
1 tsp cayenne pepper
1 tsp ground coriander
1 tsp ground cinnamon
1 tsp mustard seeds
1 tbsp olive oil
1 onion, peeled and diced
5-cm lump of ginger root, peeled and grated
2 x 400-g tins of brown lentils, rinsed

Raita
1 small cucumber, grated and squeezed with your hands
   to remove excess moisture
small bunch of fresh mint, chopped
300 g Greek yoghurt

To serve
lemon wedges
handful of baby spinach
handful of cherry tomatoes, chopped

To make the marinade, combine all the ingredients together in a large bowl. Add the salmon fillets and coat the flesh in the marinade, leaving the skin clean. Cover and refrigerate for 30 minutes if you have time.

To make the spiced lentils, place all the spices in a frying pan over medium heat and toast for 1 minute, or until they smell nutty. Add the olive oil, onion and ginger and sauté for 3–5 minutes until the onion has softened, then tumble in the lentils and stir to warm them through.

To cook the salmon, take the fillets out of the marinade bowl and sprinkle the skin generously with salt to help stop it sticking to the pan. Heat the olive oil in a frying pan over medium heat (or use a barbecue) and place the fillets, skin side down, in the pan. Cook for 3 minutes, then flip the fillets over and cook them for 2–3 minutes on the other side – most of the exterior of the salmon should be opaque except for about 1 cm halfway down. Inside, it will be gently blushing at its centre, so if you prefer your salmon well done, cook it on the second side for an extra 2 minutes. Allow the salmon to rest for 2–3 minutes before serving.

To make the raita, combine the ingredients together.

Serve the salmon on the lentils with a cheek of lemon for squeezing over the top, the spinach, cherry tomatoes and the raita on the side.

MOROCCAN LAMB AND CHICKPEA BURGERS IN LETTUCE LEAVES

Makes 8 small burgers, or serves 4

Can you really get the joy of a burger without the bun? I hazard that with these, you can. It helps that there are smooshed pulses in the patties, which are responsible for transforming this into a more sustaining supper than just mere meat and leaves. It's the kick of spices and sprightly mint-yoghurt dressing which also completes their appeal. I like to eat these with some blistered tomatoes and a cool glass of pink wine, preferably with my toes dangling in a swimming pool.

250 g cherry tomatoes
2 tbsp olive oil
1 x 400-g tin of chickpeas, rinsed
2 garlic cloves, peeled and grated
1 tbsp ground cumin
1 tbsp ground coriander
1 tsp ground cinnamon
1 tsp ground ginger
½ tsp cayenne pepper
1 egg, lightly beaten
1½ tsp sea salt
500 g lamb mince

Mint-yoghurt dressing
150 g Greek yoghurt
handful of fresh mint leaves, torn
2 tbsp olive oil

To serve
8 large leaves of soft lettuce
harissa or chilli sauce

Preheat the oven to 150°C/300°F/Gas 2.

Put the tomatoes in a roasting tray, drizzle with half of the olive oil and roast in the preheated oven for 40 minutes.

In the meantime, put three-quarters of the chickpeas, the garlic, spices, egg and salt in a food processor and blitz to a paste.

Combine the chickpea paste with the lamb mince and remaining whole chickpeas. Divide the mixture into 8 portions and shape into fat discs between your hands. Put them on a plate, cover and refrigerate for 15–30 minutes to firm up.

Heat the remaining olive oil in a frying pan (or use a barbecue) over medium heat. Fry the burgers for 3–4 minutes on each side until the outside is burnished and the inside cooked medium–rare, if that's how you like it.

To make the mint-yoghurt dressing, muddle all the ingredients together.

Serve the burgers in lettuce leaves with the roasted cherry tomatoes, mint-yoghurt dressing, and harissa or chilli sauce, to taste.

MEDITERRANEAN SQUID STUFFED WITH WHITE BEAN PURÉE AND OLIVES

Serves 2 generously

The immigration form to enter Malta lists eight check boxes of possible reasons for your visit. This is a problem. Not one of them mentions pastizzi. These small, brittle pastries stuffed with cheese became my undoing over three days on this island in the Mediterranean. That's until I discovered their version of braised octopus, stuffat tal-qarnit, cooked long and slow with tomatoes, olives and onion. What follows is a meal which combines the flavours of that dish, with a little extra ballast. The cleaned squid tubes are chocked with cannellini beans and prawns, bringing a double dose of the sea. You'll need some cocktail sticks to fasten the stuffed tubes closed and a little bit of dexterity. Hopefully this is a fish dish so satisfying you won't need to go in search of flaky pastries for a while, but if you're hankering for something sweet, try pairing it with the Baked Ricotta-Stuffed Peaches on page 162.

2 tbsp olive oil
a pinch of dried chilli flakes
3 garlic cloves, peeled and sliced
1 onion, peeled and finely diced
4 medium or 8 small squid tubes (around 225 g in total), cleaned, plus tentacles reserved if you have them
400 ml tomato passata
1x 400-g tin of cannellini beans, drained
8 small, raw, peeled prawns (50 g), diced
2 handfuls of fresh flat-leaf parsley, chopped
10 black olives, pitted and finely chopped

To serve
salad of baby spinach leaves, shaved fennel and shaved courgette, dressed in olive oil and lemon juice

Equipment
8 cocktail sticks

Put the olive oil, chilli flakes, garlic and onion in a large heavy-based saucepan or casserole dish over medium heat. Sauté for 5–7 minutes until the onion has softened. Add the squid tentacles if you have them and sauté until they tighten and take on a little colour. Pour in the tomato passata and bring to a gentle simmer, then place the lid on the pan.

Prepare the filling for the squid. Mash the cannellini beans into a rustic paste. Stir in the prawns, three-quarters of the parsley, and the olives.

Stuff the filling into the squid tubes, pushing it all the way down into the tips, and fasten the base with a cocktail stick.

Place the stuffed squids into the simmering tomato sauce. Place the lid back on and cook at a gentle simmer for 40 minutes – the squid should be opaque and the prawns in the filling cooked through.

Serve the squid with the remaining parsley and the spinach, fennel and courgette salad.

PEACH PULLED PORK
WITH DIRTY QUINOA

Serves 4–6

Pulled pork should traditionally be eaten on a white roll so fluffy it could stand in for a duvet. What we need is something else to soak up the sticky juice and to act as a foil for the soft threads of meat. Dirty rice is one option. Cajun in origin, it traditionally melds the murk of chicken liver with rice. Here we can imitate its dark complexity with a few shades of quinoa, some lentils and a hit of spice (though if you fancy adding in some ground chicken livers, go ahead). With the tacky sweetness of the peaches, this is a dish that cries out for some sharp cut-through – a slaw of cabbage dressed in apple cider vinegar would be one way, as would a piquant hot sauce. What is not negotiable is a napkin. This isn't clean eating, by any sense of the word.

1 tbsp ground cumin
1 tbsp ground coriander
1 tsp chilli powder
½ tbsp sea salt
grated zest and juice of 1 small orange
1 kg well-marbled pork shoulder, cut into pieces the size
 of a matchbook
2 tbsp olive oil
4 ripe peaches, pitted and chopped, or 220 g drained tinned
 peach halves
375 ml ginger ale (or water)
sea salt

Dirty quinoa
85 g white quinoa, rinsed
85 g red or black quinoa, rinsed
375 ml chicken stock
1 tbsp ground cumin
1 x 400-g tin of brown lentils, rinsed
handful of fresh coriander, chopped

To serve
piquant hot sauce and/or cabbage slaw

Mix together the spices, ½ tbsp salt and the orange zest and tumble the pork pieces in it.

Heat the olive oil in a large, heavy-based saucepan or casserole dish over high heat and add half the meat. Brown the meat all over, then remove it from the pan and do the same with the second half of the meat. Return all the meat to the pan with the orange juice and peaches. Add just enough ginger ale to cover the meat (topping up with water if you need more liquid). Bring the liquid to a rolling boil, then reduce it to a simmer and cook, uncovered, for 2 hours.

After 2 hours, check the meat. There should only be about a 5-mm depth of liquid left in the pan and the meat should easily shred with 2 forks. Depending on the amount of marbling in the meat, it might need a further 30 minutes or so.

About 20 minutes before serving, make the dirty quinoa. Put the quinoa, chicken stock and cumin in a saucepan and bring it to the boil, then reduce the heat. Simmer with the lid on for 15 minutes, or until most of the liquid has been absorbed. Fold through the drained lentils, season with salt and top with the coriander.

When the pork is ready, shred it with 2 forks and toss it with the remaining juices.

Serve the pork with the dirty quinoa and some piquant hot sauce – and if you fancy, a slaw of shredded cabbage dressed with apple cider vinegar.

PIRI PIRI CHICKEN WITH BLACK BEANS AND TOMATOES

Serves 4 (with enough marinade
to freeze half for another time)

This could be a story about how when we went to Portugal we ate terrific piri piri chicken. Except it's not. Lisbon in late June is not for the faint-hearted. It's searingly hot, the kind of heat where the pavement seems to warp from the beating beams of glare. The air is soupish and the only place you want to be is in the water, or the shade doing nothing more energetic than chasing stray drips off an ice cream. I'm sure if we looked properly we might have found the quarter of chicken, charred and blistered with peppers, oregano, citrus and acids that we hoped for. Except we didn't. On our final day we resorted to eating salt cod with a side dish of mild disappointment. It wasn't until we returned home to London that I realised we didn't need to be in Portugal to have the chicken we dreamed of. All we needed were some spices, some patience – and a strong pair of scissors.

a 1.8–2-kg chicken
250 g cherry tomatoes
2 x 400-g tins of black beans, rinsed
3 double handfuls of kale, roughly chopped
6 marinated red peppers, drained and diced
Aïoli (page 42), to serve

Piri piri marinade
1 small red onion, peeled and cut into rough chunks
3 garlic cloves, peeled
125 ml olive oil
60 ml red wine vinegar
1–2 chillies (deseeded if you don't like things too spicy)
1 red pepper, deseeded and roughly chopped
1 tbsp paprika
½ tbsp dried oregano
grated zest and juice of ½ lemon
a pinch of sea salt
dried chilli flakes or chilli powder, to taste (optional)
brown sugar, to taste (optional)

Preheat the oven to 200°C/400°F/Gas 6.

To make the marinade, blitz all the ingredients together in a food processor until smooth. Taste and adjust the flavouring – if you like more heat, add chilli flakes or some chilli powder; if it's too acrid, add a little brown sugar. The sweetness and the heat will depend on which peppers, chillies and red wine vinegar you use. You want a balance of warmth and vinegar.

Transfer the marinade to a frying pan over medium heat and sauté it for 5–7 minutes to thicken it, stirring frequently. Set it aside to cool slightly.

To cut the backbone out of the chicken, the easiest method is with some kitchen scissors. Once it's been removed, splay the chicken out onto a board and press it down to flatten it. Pour half the marinade over the chicken and massage it into the skin. Reserve or freeze the other half of the marinade.

Place the chicken in a roasting tray with the cherry tomatoes. Bake it in the preheated oven for about 45–50 minutes, or until the chicken breast reaches 73°C/164°F internally and the juices in the leg of the chicken run clear when you prick it with a knife.

Leave the chicken to rest while you prepare the vegetables. Put the black beans, kale, roasted cherry tomatoes and marinated peppers in a saucepan over medium heat and stir until the beans are warm and the kale has wilted.

Carve the chicken and serve it with the warmed vegetables, a little extra sauce from the roasting tray and some Aïoli on the side.

TIP: *It's well worth it to spatchcock the chicken. It allows the marinade to cover much more of the surface of the bird. It also allows the chicken to cook more swiftly.*

Is it possible to have comfort food with fewer carbs? Yes. It is. Whether it's gnocchi made from white beans, or the edible hug which is a blue cheese soufflé, all it takes is a few sneaky tricks here and there to turn the food that you crave on duvet days into stuff that still makes you feel good. Whether it's using chickpea flour in a béchamel, omitting the potatoes from your choucroute or stuffing cabbage rolls with a combination of quinoa, mince and mushrooms, there are plenty of ways to make your winter warmers a little lighter.

This is the sort of food I want to make again and again when the wind is whipping and I'm searching for an excuse to turn the oven on. We'll raid the pantry and settle in with lentil meatballs with ajvar, or a lamb and fig tagine. We'll turn on the television. Occasionally we'll get to huddle by a fire. We may even get around to cracking a good bottle of red. Winter may be coming, but it doesn't have to be that bleak.

HUDDLE-BY-THE-FIRE COMFORT FOOD

BLUE CHEESE SOUFFLÉS

Serves 4

There is some unnecessary stigma surrounding soufflés. If you can make a white sauce and whip an egg white, you can make one. Sure there are some tips to ease the way – using room-temperature eggs will give a better rise, as will cooling the cheesy béchamel before you fold in the stiff whites. I tend to get the best results when I cook them on the lowest shelf of the oven (and then take them straight to the table, though don't fret too much, as it's in their nature to slouch when you serve them – a rumpled crown is part of the appeal). As light as the air is in these, the blue cheese makes them rather plush. Placing some plumes of radicchio on the side helps with cut-through, providing both a bitter contrast and an excellent device for dunking. I find one small portion of the soufflés is sufficient; any more can feel more onerous than indulgent. To round out the meal try serving them with the Chickpeas, Leek, Apple and Pear Salad on page 75 for additional crunch and contrast.

40 g butter, plus extra for greasing
2 tbsp ground almonds or hazelnuts
40 g chickpea (besan or gram) flour
225 ml milk
150 g blue cheese
½ tbsp fresh thyme leaves
4 egg whites
sea salt and freshly ground black pepper
radicchio leaves, to serve

Equipment
4 x 250-ml ramekins or small copper pots

Preheat the oven to 180°C/350°F/Gas 4.

Lightly grease the ramekins or copper pots with butter. Pour the ground nuts into the base of one and shake it to coat the sides with the nuts, then pour the excess into the next ramekin or pot and repeat until they have all been dusted.

Place a saucepan over medium heat. Add the butter and leave it to melt, then add the flour and stir it to create a paste. Cook the paste for 2 minutes, or until it has turned a light brown.

Gradually pour in the milk, whisking it with a balloon whisk until it thickens to a gloopy white sauce like béchamel. Add the cheese and thyme and stir until the cheese has melted and the mixture is smooth. Remove the pan from the heat, season the mixture with salt and pepper and allow it to cool for at least 5 minutes.

In a clean bowl, use an electric whisk to beat the egg whites with a pinch of salt until soft peaks form. Fold the egg whites into the cheese mixture in 3 batches, trying not to knock too much air out, until everything is just combined.

Portion the soufflé batter into the prepared ramekins or pots, filling them just three-quarters full, and place them on a baking tray on the bottom shelf of the preheated oven. Bake them for 25 minutes until puffed up and golden brown.

Serve the soufflés immediately with radicchio leaves for dipping, and potentially the Chickpeas, Leek, Apple and Pear Salad on page 75.

TIP: *You could easily substitute the blue cheese for crumbled goats' cheese or gratings of a good English Cheddar. If you're looking for a way to use up your leftover egg yolks, try the passionfruit curd on page 161, perhaps substituting the zest and juice of a clementine to give it a wintry twist. The curd is lovely layered with yoghurt as a light dessert.*

BAKED WHITE-BEAN GNOCCHI WITH MEATBALLS, MOZZARELLA AND TOMATO

Serves 2

To me, potato gnocchi are the greatest comfort food of all, and one of the things I was saddest to let go of when I tried to curb my carb addiction. Then I began musing – is it possible to make gnocchi from pulses?

The answer is yes. And while purists may roll their eyes, it has the added benefit of being the quickest and easiest gnocchi I've ever made. It's two tins of white beans, drained and rinsed, then blitzed with a stick blender. That's something you can't do with potatoes, unless you want to use the resulting purée to hold up wallpaper. If I'm craving really fluffy gnocchi I'll work the purée through a strainer or a mouli. This helps get out all errant lumps and incorporate as much air as possible. I'll acknowledge, this isn't completely carb-free, but it's not the double excesses of potato and flour that you'll find in the original. The extra protein in the beans will make them a little sturdier than potato gnocchi, but when baked they possess a very pleasing contrast of external crunch to inside squish.

sea salt and freshly ground black pepper

Gnocchi
2 x 400-g tins butter or cannellini beans, rinsed
   (leaving 440 g beans when drained)
1 egg yolk
100 g plain or '00' white wheat flour, plus extra for dusting
olive oil, for drizzling

Sauce
300 g cherry tomatoes
1 tbsp olive oil
200 g beef or pork mince
1 tsp dried oregano
3 tbsp tomato paste (more if the tomatoes aren't as juicy
   as you hoped)
a pinch of sugar
300 g buffalo mozzarella, roughly torn
fresh basil or oregano leaves, to garnish

Equipment
baking tray lined with baking paper
ovenproof dish, the size of an A4 sheet of paper

Preheat the oven to 180°C/350°F/Gas 4. For the gnocchi, purée the beans using a stick blender or food processor until completely smooth. For the best results, pass the purée through a sieve, strainer or mouli. Put the purée, egg yolk and a good pinch of salt in a large bowl. Sift the flour in, bit by bit, and use one hand to lightly and gently bring it together into a dough. Don't work it too hard otherwise it will become tough.

Dust a clean bench with a little more flour. Divide the dough into 4 balls. Hold your hands out, flat, on top of one portion of dough. Press it as though you were pushing a piece of paper away from you and then pulling it back towards you to roll the dough into a long rope as thick as a wine cork. Set it aside and repeat with the remaining 3 balls of dough.

Line the dough ropes up next to each other and simultaneously cut all 4 into gnocchi around 1.5 cm long. (Lining the ropes up next to each other will help create equal-sized gnocchi.) Place the gnocchi on the lined baking tray, drizzle lightly with olive oil and bake in the preheated oven for 20 minutes. This helps the gnocchi to set so they don't get too slimy when they are baked in the sauce later on.

Reduce the oven temperature to 150°C/300°F/Gas 2. For the sauce, put the cherry tomatoes in the ovenproof dish, drizzle with the olive oil and sprinkle with a pinch of salt. Bake in the oven for 20 minutes, or until the tomatoes have softened and wrinkled.

While the tomatoes are roasting, make the meatballs. Combine the meat with the dried oregano, a pinch of salt, a good grinding of black pepper and 1 tablespoon of very cold water. Squash it all together with your hands, and then portion the mixture into meatballs the same size as the cherry tomatoes. When the tomatoes have been in the oven for 20 minutes, add the meatballs to the dish and pop the dish back in the oven for another 20 minutes.

When the tomatoes are roasted, bloated and softened from the oven, squash them with a fork to encourage the innards to ooze out and make a sauce. Add the tomato paste and sugar and stir gently. Nestle the gnocchi in amongst the meatballs and the tomatoes. You want to make sure that there is enough liquid from the busted tomatoes to come at least halfway up the sides of the gnocchi. If not, add another 1–2 tablespoons tomato paste muddled with a little water, or make up the shortfall with tomato passata.

Top with the well drained and torn mozzarella and bake for 30 minutes, or until the cheese has melted and browned and the gnocchi are cooked through.

Serve the baked gnocchi with basil or oregano on top.

CHOUCROUTE

Serves 6

An Alsatian speciality involving the tang of sauerkraut and the smokey intensity of pork, choucroute is often served with potatoes. I first realised that they were extraneous to the experience beneath the vaulted ceiling of London's The Delaunay. I was more than happy to leave my perfectly turned tubers to the side to save room for a slice of torte. Since that day, I've never missed them. At the outset, choucroute may seem involved, but it's really more of an assembly job, since the sauerkraut and sausages come ready formed. Be sure not to omit the apples and juniper berries – they provide the necessary floral notes to balance the acidity of the cabbage. Beyond that, a variety of mustards on the table to share will help pull the fattiness of the pork into line. Add a lager or two, or a nice bottle of Riesling, and you've got the makings of a proper celebration. (And if you're looking for a fitting treat with which to finish the meal, try the Salzburger Nockerl on page 158 or the Black Forest notes of the Chocolate, Black Bean and Cherry Cake on page 164).

700 g sauerkraut in brine
1 tbsp olive oil
800 g good-quality pork sausages
3 onions, peeled and diced
2 medium carrots, peeled and diced
1 garlic clove, peeled and grated
2 green apples, peeled, cored and grated
375 ml chicken stock
500 ml dry white wine (Riesling is classic)
1 fresh or dried bay leaf
6 black peppercorns
6 cloves
8 juniper berries
200 g thick-cut ham steaks, cut into pieces the size
  of a matchbook
400 g smoked sausage (try kielbasa, cabanossi, bratwurst)

To serve
Dijon mustard, wholegrain mustard and German mustard

Rinse the sauerkraut from its brine and set it aside to drain.

Preheat the oven to 160°C/325°F/Gas 3.

Put the olive oil in a large, flameproof and heatproof casserole dish over medium heat and add the pork sausages. Stir them until they are evenly browned, then remove them from the dish and set them aside.

In the same dish, sauté the onions and carrots for 5–7 minutes until they have softened. Add the garlic and apples and stir for 2 minutes. Add the sauerkraut, stock, wine, bay leaf, peppercorns, cloves and juniper berries and bring to a simmer.

Return the browned sausages to the dish, place the lid on, and bake in the preheated oven for 1½ hours.

Tuck the cut ham and smoked sausage into the casserole dish and replace the lid. Return to the oven and bake for another 30 minutes, or until the meats have heated through. Pluck out the bay leaf, warn your guests about the juniper berries and peppercorns, and serve the choucroute with the mustards.

AUBERGINE 'PARM'

Serves 4 (or 6 with a big green salad,
or as a side for some roast lamb, steak or fish)

This dish is half a meatless moussaka and half a pimped up 'parm'. It's also one with some secrets buried inside. It's up to you whether you want to let people in on the fact that the béchamel is bolstered by a tin of blitzed cannellini beans and an egg. They'll probably never know they're there but you'll appreciate the extra protein. The second is the use of a panini press to toast your aubergine slices. It saves on oil from frying (aubergines can be the thirstiest of nightshades) and thanks to the heat coming from both sides it will cook them in double time. There's a little bit of hands-on work in layering it all together, but the end result is something that's hearty, bubbling and very hard to just have one portion of.

3 large aubergines
3 tbsp olive oil
80 g Parmesan, shaved
150 g mozzarella
large handful of fresh basil leaves, to serve
sea salt and freshly ground black pepper

Tomato sauce
1 tbsp olive oil
1 onion, peeled and diced
2 garlic cloves, peeled and thinly sliced
2 x 400-g tins of chopped tomatoes
1 tbsp dried oregano
a pinch of dried chilli flakes (optional)

Béchamel
50 g butter
50 g chickpea (besan or gram) flour or plain wheat flour
400 ml milk
1 x 400-g tin of cannellini beans or chickpeas rinsed and
   puréed (to help create a smoother purée you can add
   2 tbsp milk or water)
1 egg, lightly beaten

Equipment
lasagne dish, 30 cm long, greased

Lop the top off the aubergines. Cut them lengthways into slices 1.5 cm thick and brush them with the olive oil.

Use a panini press or a griddle pan to 'toast' the aubergine slices in batches, until the outsides are golden brown and the insides are pliable.

Meanwhile, to make the tomato sauce, heat the olive oil in a frying pan over medium heat and sauté the onion and garlic for 5–7 minutes until they have softened, taking care not to scorch the garlic. Add the tinned tomatoes, oregano and dried chilli and bring it to a simmer. You want the sauce to cook until it is thick and chunky. Taste it: if it is a little acrid, add a teaspoon of sugar. Now is also the time to add salt to taste.

Preheat the oven to 180°C/350°F/Gas 4.

While the tomato sauce is reducing, take a separate saucepan and make the béchamel. Melt the butter over medium heat, then add the flour and stir it to create a paste. Cook the paste for 2 minutes, or until it has turned a light brown. Gradually pour in the milk, whisking it with a balloon whisk until it thickens to a nice, lump-free white sauce like béchamel. Stir in the puréed beans, then remove from the heat and stir through the egg and ½ teaspoon pepper.

Lay one-third of the grilled aubergines across the base of the prepared lasagne dish, top to tail to help fill all the corners. It can be quite rustic. Cover them with half the tomato sauce and one-third of the Parmesan and mozzarella. Layer another third of the aubergines, then cover them with the remaining tomato sauce and another third of the cheeses. Use the remaining aubergines to form a final layer.

Pour the béchamel evenly over the top, making sure to leave a few millimetres clear at the top of the dish as the sauce will rise a little with baking. Sprinkle with the remaining cheeses.

Bake the 'parm' in the preheated oven for 45 minutes, or until the top is golden and bubbling.

Serve strewn with basil leaves.

LAMB SHANK AND FIG TAGINE

Serves 4–6

Most of the tagines I ate in Marrakech were elegant trios – lamb, prune and onion, or chicken, peppers and lemon – and yet they fell flat. It may have been the heat. Stewed meats are just not what I fancy when the mercury is tipping 40˚ C. What follows is by no means a muffled braise, but a busy jumble of spices and textures. And to me this aromatic combination of slow-cooked lamb and vegetables has swiftly become the perfect wintry Sunday night supper. It's self-contained enough to justify pulling the slow cooker down from the top of the cupboard, or dusting off the casserole dish. I find that the chickpeas bobbing about in here are perfectly filling and all I need is a splash of yoghurt and a dab of harissa to make it sing. If you really crave something strapping as a base, try it with some quinoa or some plain Cauliflower 'Couscous' from page 76.

3 tbsp olive oil
4 large or 6 medium lamb shanks (or 1 kg diced lamb
　shoulder, chicken thighs or peeled sweet potato)
2 tsp sea salt
2 onions, peeled, halved and cut into slim half-moons
2 carrots, peeled and sliced
2 garlic cloves, peeled and sliced
1 tsp ground cumin
1 tsp ground coriander
1 tsp ground ginger
1 tsp ground cinnamon
a pinch of chilli powder
750 ml chicken stock
a pinch of saffron threads
1 x 400-g tin of chickpeas, rinsed
200 g dried figs, cut in half

To serve
plain yoghurt
fresh coriander
harissa or chilli sauce, to taste
quinoa or Cauliflower 'Couscous' (see page 76) (optional)

Preheat the oven to 150˚C/300˚F/Gas 2.

Put 2 tablespoons of the olive oil in a flameproof and heatproof casserole dish over medium heat. Season the lamb shanks with the salt and add them, in batches, to the casserole dish to sear them. Be careful not to overcrowd the pan. Sear them until they are evenly browned, then remove them from the dish and set them aside.

Add the remaining olive oil to the casserole dish and sauté the onions, carrots, garlic and spices (bar the saffron) for 5–7 minutes until the vegetables have begun to soften and the spices smell toasty.

Pour the chicken stock into the dish and scrape the bottom with a metal spoon to rescue any flavour that's clinging to the pot. Add the saffron, chickpeas, figs and lamb shanks, then bring the stock to a simmer. Clamp on a lid and cook in the preheated oven for 3–4 hours, until the meat is slinking off the bone and the figs are nice and soft.

Serve the tagine with yoghurt, fresh coriander, chilli sauce and quinoa or Cauliflower 'Couscous', if you need some additional fodder.

PORK, BEEF AND MUSHROOM-STUFFED CABBAGE ROLLS

Serves 4

When I married into a surname comprised of a smash of consonants, it carried with it a new world of foods. Cabbage rolls were the first through the door. They're a prized dish from the Romanian/Croatian arm of the family, and one of my husband's favourite childhood comfort foods. He first converted me to their charm by describing them as carbless cannelloni. It's half right. The Haschka family's version is made from home-pickled cabbage which sheaths a bundle of paprika-spiced mince and rice. It's the sort of food which encourages you to stand up straight and face the day with confidence. This version takes a shortcut by skipping the pickling, instead wilting the cabbage under hot water. There's also the nuttiness of quinoa in place of white rice, and some additional earthiness from the mushrooms. You can easily use veal mince for the pork, or go completely vegetarian and triple the quantity of mushrooms. We serve it with some sauerkraut for an acidic kick and a slick of sour cream or yoghurt for a bit of extra richness. I haven't quite mustered the courage to make this version for the extended family and experts yet, but one day, maybe I will.

1 whole head of savoy cabbage
1 tbsp olive oil
200 g button mushrooms, thinly sliced
1 tbsp fresh thyme leaves
150 g pork mince
150 g beef mince
1½ tbsp paprika
1 tbsp fresh flat-leaf parsley, chopped
2 garlic cloves, peeled and finely chopped
140 g cooked quinoa
1 x 680-g jar of tomato passata
sea salt and freshly ground black pepper

To serve
sauerkraut and crème fraîche or sour cream

Preheat the oven to 180°C/350°F/Gas 4 and boil some water in the kettle.

Cut the base off the cabbage, submerge in cold water and pull the outer leaves off, one by one. Place the leaves in a large saucepan and pour the boiling water over them. Allow them to soak for 2 minutes to soften, then refresh them under cold water.

Put the olive oil in a saucepan over medium heat and sauté the mushrooms and thyme until the mushrooms have browned. Set aside to cool.

Mix together the meats, 1 tablespoon of the paprika, the parsley, garlic, and cooled mushrooms and thyme. Season well with salt and pepper. Fold through the cooked quinoa and mix well to combine.

Pour half the tomato passata into a casserole dish and set aside.

To assemble the cabbage rolls, first cut out and discard the tough stem from the centre of the blanched cabbage leaves.

Place 1½–2 tablespoons of the filling in the centre of each leaf. Roll the top of the leaf down over the filling, then tuck in the 2 sides and continue rolling until you have a neat little parcel. Set the roll aside, seam side down, and repeat the process with the remaining leaves and filling.

Nestle the rolls, seam side down, on the passata in the casserole dish. Pour the remaining passata over the top and sprinkle with the remaining paprika. Place the lid on the dish and bake in the preheated oven for 1 hour.

After 1 hour, remove the lid and bake for another 30 minutes to help the sauce to reduce and thicken.

Serve the cabbage rolls with sauerkraut and a splodge of crème fraîche or sour cream.

LENTIL 'MEATBALLS' WITH AJVAR AND TOMATO

Makes 14–16 'meatballs',
or serves 2 generously, or 4 with a large salad

Ajvar is a Balkan secret weapon in the kitchen. It's a robust relish made from roasted peppers and garlic. Its piquancy makes it perfect with grilled meats – most often we've enjoyed it on the side of a simple mixed grill. I'm happy to report that it also makes a novel sauce for 'meatballs'. These small spheres of lentils are an excellent stand-in on Meatless Mondays – and filling enough for you to easily forgo any pasta or mashed potato as a base. Just add some flat-leaf parsley and a little sour cream to the top before serving, though a big green salad and some pickles on the side are also great.

2 x 400-g tins of brown lentils, rinsed
2 tbsp finely grated Parmesan
1 tbsp tomato paste
1 egg, lightly beaten
2 tbsp fresh flat-leaf parsley, finely chopped,
  plus extra to serve
1 tbsp Hungarian paprika
a pinch of sea salt
chickpea (besan or gram) or wholemeal plain wheat flour
  (optional)
2 tbsp olive oil

Sauce
550 g ajvar (Balkan red pepper relish)
200 g cherry tomatoes

To serve
4 tbsp crème fraîche or sour cream
green salad
pickles

Equipment
baking tray lined with baking paper

Using a stick blender or food processor, blend four-fifths of the lentils until smooth. Fold in the remaining lentils, the Parmesan, tomato paste, egg, parsley, paprika and salt. The mixture should hold together like cookie dough but if it is too wet and droopy, you can rescue it by adding 1–2 tablespoons chickpea or wholemeal flour. Portion the mixture into meatballs the same size as golf balls. They will get a little mucky. Place them on the lined baking tray and refrigerate them for 30 minutes to firm up.

Preheat the oven to 180°C/350°F/Gas 4.

After 30 minutes, drizzle the meatballs with the olive oil and transfer the baking tray to the preheated oven. Bake for 25–30 minutes until they have browned.

In the meantime, for the sauce, put the ajvar and tomatoes in a saucepan over medium heat until the tomatoes have softened and popped and the ajvar has heated through.

Serve the meatballs on the sauce, glossed with a little crème fraîche or sour cream and some parsley. Eat with a green salad and some pickles on the side.

TIP: *Ajvar is available in the international foods section of many supermarkets, or from the Macedonian ingredients website pelagonia.co.uk. Otherwise you can fashion your own by blending together a 500-g jar of drained roasted red peppers with a garlic clove, 2 tsp olive oil and 1 tsp red wine vinegar.*

THYME-ROASTED CHICKEN LEGS WITH BRAISED BABY LETTUCE AND PEAS

Serves 2 generously

This is not so much a recipe as a formula for dinner-party success, even if what you're hosting is just an intimate meal for two. One of the most sympathetic and indestructible pieces of meat to cook is a chicken leg with the thigh still attached. Here you get the perfect mix of crisp skin and dark meat without the faff of trying to carve a bird in front of company. All you need to do is season them and shut the oven for 40 minutes and they'll be golden every time. What you want then is a low-maintenance side dish that does most of its work in tandem. The answer lies in a tasty trivet. This base of flavours will benefit from the roasting juices that seep down from the bird, while helping to lift it up. To me the combination of lardons, onion and garlic are perfect. While the legs are resting, that trio becomes the backbone of a French-accented dish of peas with sweet braised and shredded lettuce. It's a tactic that travels well. If it's Spain that beckons, replace the lardons with chorizo and throw some cherry tomatoes and smoked paprika in with the greens. If it's Italy, then switch the thyme for oregano and use cavolo nero instead of lettuce. And if it's more of an Asian sojourn you're after, then lob in some lap cheong (Chinese sausage) for lardons and pull into play some wilted Chinese greens.

90 g lardons or smoked bacon, finely chopped
2 small–medium onions, peeled, halved and sliced
  into half-moons
3 garlic cloves, peeled and grated
2 chicken leg and thigh joints
2 tsp fresh thyme leaves
1 tsp sea salt flakes
Dijon mustard, to serve

Braised lettuce and peas
2 gem lettuces, cored and very finely shredded
260 g frozen peas
125 ml white wine

Preheat the oven to 180°C/350°F/Gas 4.

Line a baking tray with the lardons, onions and garlic – this is the 'trivet' that forms the base of the dish and provides all the flavour. Sprinkle the top of the chicken legs with the thyme and salt, then place them on the trivet in the baking tray. Bake in the preheated oven for 40 minutes, or until the juices from the thigh joint run clear.

Remove the chicken from the baking tray and set it aside somewhere warm to rest.

For the braised lettuce and peas, transfer the trivet and all the chicken juices to a large saucepan or casserole dish over high heat and fry to ensure all the fat on the bacon has rendered. Add the lettuce, peas and wine and braise over medium heat until the lettuce has wilted and the peas are warmed through.

Serve the chicken over the braised lettuce and peas with a dab of Dijon mustard.

<u>TIP:</u> *It should go without saying that in all of this, buying free-range and organic chicken legs will make all the difference to the end result.*

PRAWN AND QUINOA GRITS

Serves 2 generously

Shrimps cooked in bacon grease and bobbing across a lake of grits is about as Southern as y'all can get. These puddles of hominy are almost a kissing cousin of semolina and polenta and the true definition of rib-sticking sustenance. Yet if it's treated with a little extra love and attention, you can get a similar squelching appeal (but lighter effect) from gussied-up quinoa. Gloss it with a little cream cheese for ooze and add in some lemon zest for lift. If you cook the quinoa in chicken stock it will also help boost the flavours – though if you're after an extra kick, try roasting the shells of your prawns for 15 minutes in a moderate oven and infusing them in the warm chicken stock for 20 minutes. This may be a classic breakfast during a Southern summer when prawns are in season but I find it's also a heart-warming dinner in winter – and a great way to revive any crustaceans you've stashed in the freezer.

190 g quinoa, rinsed
500 ml chicken stock
2 tbsp cream cheese
½ lemon
1 tbsp butter
1 tbsp olive oil
1 red chilli, finely chopped
6 spring onions, white and green bits finely chopped
2 garlic cloves, peeled and thinly sliced
100 g (2 slices) smoked streaky bacon, cut into small batons
500 g raw prawns, peeled, and heads and digestive tracts removed (300 g peeled weight)
piquant hot sauce, to serve (optional)

Put the quinoa and chicken stock in a saucepan and bring it to the boil, then reduce the heat. Simmer with the lid on for 15 minutes, or until most of the liquid has been absorbed. Stir through the cream cheese, and grate in the zest from the lemon half (and then reserve the lemon half). You want a slightly droopy consistency, so if it is too tight, add more cream cheese or a slosh of hot water.

While the quinoa is cooking, put a large frying pan over medium heat and add the butter, olive oil, half of the chilli, white bits of the spring onions, garlic and bacon. Add the reserved lemon half, cut side down, in the pan. Cook until the bacon has begun to render its fat and take on some colour.

Add the prawns and cook for 3–4 minutes until they have turned nicely pink. Remove them from the pan.

Squeeze the burnished lemon into the pan and scrape up any colour that has clung to bottom to create a rustic sauce. Serve the prawns over the quinoa, topped with the bacon and pan juices. Top with the remaining chilli, the piquant hot sauce, if you like, and a handful of the green bits from the spring onions.

SAUSAGES WITH LEEKS, CARAMELISED ONIONS, MUSHROOMS AND BEANS

Serves 4

This is a dish borne from a frosty afternoon of fridge foraging. Sausages, onion, leek and mushrooms were what were left in the kitchen one day when Baby Will was just three weeks old. I couldn't bring myself to drag the pram outside into the cold to fetch anything more. I was also hunting for any excuse to turn the oven on to steal some chill from the air. It turned into the happiest of coincidences. By baking the sausages and mushrooms I ended up with crisp edges to contrast with the silky softness of the leeks and the onions, while the creamed beans tied it all together. The end result is a perfectly homely dish, best consumed from bowls on the couch, while a wee one who's wrapped up in a bunny rug snuffles and grunts like an old man beside you.

250 g button mushrooms, halved

400 g small pork or beef sausages

3 tbsp olive oil

1 red onion, peeled, halved and cut into slim half-moons

1 leek, green parts trimmed and discarded, remainder rinsed and sliced into coins 5 mm thick

125 ml water

1 tsp Dijon mustard

2 x 400-g tins of cannellini beans, rinsed

1 tsp grated nutmeg

2 handfuls of baby spinach

sea salt and freshly ground black pepper

3 tbsp crème fraîche, to serve

Preheat the oven to 180°C/350°F/Gas 4.

Put the mushrooms and sausages in a large flameproof and heatproof casserole dish, drizzle with 1 tablespoon of the olive oil and bake in the preheated oven for about 30 minutes.

In the meantime, put the remaining olive oil in a frying pan over medium heat and sauté the onion and leek for 20 minutes, stirring occasionally, until they have softened and taken on a golden hue.

Using a stick blender or food processor, blitz together the water, mustard and 1 tin of the beans until you have a smooth purée.

Add the softened onion and leek, roasted mushrooms and sausages, second tin of beans, bean purée, nutmeg and spinach into the casserole dish and place on the hob over low heat until the spinach wilts. Season with salt and pepper to taste and top with the crème fraîche before serving.

MISO AUBERGINE WITH GINGER TOFU AND ADZUKI BEANS

Serves 2–3

The appeal of nasu dengaku is largely textural: it's hard to turn away from a plinth of scored aubergine capped with a glaze of sticky miso. What it needs to transform it from a winning snack to a proper meal is some substance. Enter adzuki beans. Adzuki beans may physically resemble black beans, but their taste is milder and naturally sweeter. Cook them in the same pot in which you made your glaze and you'll end up with a terrific tumble of taste and texture. I find if I add a small rectangle of grilled tofu and a salad of raw mangetout and cucumber dressed with yuzu, I've got all bases covered. Remember, one joy of miso paste is that it's already fermented and won't go off, so it's well worth keeping some tucked in the fridge in a Tupperware for when you need a quick meal.

2 medium or 1 large aubergine
2 tbsp neutral-tasting oil
5 tbsp white (shiro) miso
2-cm lump of ginger root, peeled and grated
1 tsp toasted sesame oil
2 tsp brown or muscovado sugar
4 tbsp mirin rice wine
1 x 400-g tin of adzuki beans, rinsed
200 g firm tofu, drained and cut into 2 steaks
2 spring onions, white and green bits finely chopped
1 tbsp black sesame seeds
salad of raw mangetout and cucumber, to serve

Preheat the oven to 200°C/400°F/Gas 6.

Lop the tops off the aubergines, then cut them into thirds, lengthways. Score the aubergine slices a few times with the tip of a sharp knife, taking care not to cut all the way through to the bottom. Brush them with the neutral-tasting oil and place them on a baking tray. Roast them in the preheated oven for 35–40 minutes, until the slices are tender when pierced.

While the aubergines are roasting, put the miso, ginger, sesame oil, sugar, and 3 tablespoons of the mirin in a saucepan over medium heat. Whisk to combine and allow it to warm up.

When the aubergines are ready, switch the oven over to grill mode and turn it up to high.

Paint the scored tops of the aubergine slices with the miso mixture and put them back on the baking tray. Add the beans to the pan you made the miso mixture in and warm them over low heat.

Nestle the tofu slices in and around the aubergine slices on the tray and drizzle them with the remaining mirin. Top with the white bits of the spring onions. Place the tray under the grill and grill until the miso topping is bronzed and bubbling and the tofu is lightly tanned.

Serve the grilled tofu and aubergine on the beans and topped with the sesame seeds and the green bits of the spring onions. Accompany with a mangetout and cucumber salad.

TIP. *For this dish, be sure to have the palest 'shiro'/white miso you can find. The regular brown miso will be too savoury for the right balance of flavours here.*

DUCK BREASTS WITH ROAST BEETROOT, RADISH AND COCOA

Serves 4

Apart from their unique ability to stain everything in the kitchen when peeled, beetroot are special things. When roasted in their skins, protected under a canopy of foil, they become lolly-sweet. On their own they'd be fine. But believe me when I say the mild bitterness of a puckered radish and a grating of dark chocolate really make them shine. Beetroot and cocoa have long been friends – the internet is teeming with accounts of their joint escapades in brownies, whoopie pies and cake pops. Here the darkest chocolate adds some murky intrigue to a warm salad which becomes festively fabulous with duck breasts – and for those in the southern hemisphere it will do the same for char-grilled fillets of kangaroo. Either way, you've got a feast that's worth risking a little bit of tainted skin for.

bunch of fresh, medium beetroots (about 10 in total) –
   it's lovely if you can get varying colours
bunch of radishes (about 10 in total)
2 tbsp olive oil
1 tbsp salt
20 g very dark chocolate (minimum 70% cocoa solids,
   but 85–90% is best), finely grated
4 medium duck breasts, skin on and trimmed of sinew
2 tbsp blanched hazelnuts, toasted
sea salt and freshly ground black pepper

Preheat the oven to 200°C/400°F/Gas 6.

Wash the beetroots and radishes to remove any dirt and trim the stalks to leave a few centimetres tufting out of the top. Take 2 radishes, shave them into slivers on a mandolin or with a vegetable peeler and put them in a bowl of cold water to stay crisp.

You want all the beetroots and remaining radishes to be around the same size. If some are much bigger, cut them in half to ensure a more even cooking time. Aim for no larger than a golf ball. Scatter them on a baking tray.

Drizzle the beetroots and radishes with the olive oil and season with 1 tablespoon salt. Cover the tray with foil and bake in the preheated oven for 1½–2 hours until a skewer easily slides through the centre.

When the vegetables are done, remove them from the oven and leave the oven on. Allow the vegetables to cool slightly, then rub the skins off the beetroots – it's best to wear rubber gloves when you do this!

Sprinkle the chocolate over the top of the roasted vegetables. Season with a little extra salt and pepper.

Score lines in the skin of the duck breasts using a small, sharp knife, being careful not to cut all the way through to the flesh underneath. Season the scored skin with salt. Place 2 duck breasts, skin side down, in a cold frying pan and set over the highest heat. When you hear the fat start to sizzle, cook for 4 minutes. Remove them from the pan, set aside, clean out the pan and repeat the cooking process with the other 2 duck breasts.

Transfer all the duck breasts to the oven and cook for 5 minutes for rare, and 8 minutes or longer if you like things cooked through.

Allow the duck to rest for 5 minutes before carving it into thick slices. Serve with the roasted vegetables, toasted hazelnuts and raw radish slivers.

WHITE-BEAN COLCANNON WITH STICKY BRAISED BEEF

Serves 4–6 with a salad

Trying to win some friends over to a spudless way of eating can be hard graft. You may struggle to convince a Dubliner that a colcannon made from white beans is worth their time. But the humble cabbage – in this case the deep emerald hues of kale – has proved it can still be a star when folded through any mass of mash, whether potato or pulse. This version of colcannon is an excellent complement for many family basics; from sausages with slow-cooked onion gravy, pork chops with apple sauce to sticky slow-cooked beef stews. This braised beef is a no-fuss sort of supper. Start the stew in the morning and let it blip away all afternoon. The end result is bold and confident, calming and comforting all at once.

sea salt and freshly ground black pepper

Sticky braised beef

2 tbsp olive oil

150 g lardons or bacon cut into slim strips

1 kg chuck steak or beef shin with a good amount of white sinew marbled through, cut into 2-cm cubes (avoid a lean cut as it will turn to leather over long cooking)

3 medium carrots, peeled, halved lengthways and cut into 1-cm thick slices

2 onions, peeled, halved and cut into slim half-moons

300 g button mushrooms, halved

3 garlic cloves, peeled and finely diced

500 ml beef stock

3 tbsp Worcestershire sauce

White-bean colcannon

2 x 400-g tins of white beans, rinsed

30 ml milk

100 g kale, washed and finely chopped

5 spring onions, trimmed and thinly sliced

chopped fresh flat-leaf parsley, to serve

Start with the sticky braised beef. Preheat the oven to 150°C/300°F/Gas 2.

Add half of the olive oil to a flameproof and heatproof casserole dish over medium heat and sauté the lardons or bacon until they have browned and rendered their fat. Remove from the dish.

Season the beef chunks with 1 teaspoon salt. Brown them in small batches in the dish, making sure you get a good brown crust on the meat, as this is the basis of much of the flavour in the braise. If you crowd the pan, the meat will limply stew rather than crisply sear – you don't want this. When the meat is brown all over, remove it from the dish and set it aside. Repeat with the remaining beef and if the dish ever seems too dry, add a little more olive oil.

Once all the meat is done, add the remaining olive oil, then the carrots, onions, mushrooms and garlic (it's fine if there is some residue from the meat clinging to the bottom). Sauté for 5–10 minutes over medium heat to soften the vegetables a little and to add a hint of colour.

Return the bacon and meat (and any juices that have leached out) into the dish. Stir to combine, then pour in the stock and Worcestershire sauce. There should be enough liquid to just come to the top of the meat. If it doesn't, add some more stock or water so that the majority of the stew is covered, but some bits pop out the top like floating islands.

Turn the heat up to high and allow the stock to come to the boil. As soon as it comes to the boil, take the pan off the heat, put the lid on and place in the preheated oven for 2 hours.

After 2 hours, take off the lid and bake for another hour. This will help the sauce to reduce.

When done, the meat should flake apart, the carrots and onions should be pliable and soft and the sauce sticky and rich. If you're not quite at that point, return the stew to the oven. You could also cook this on low in a slow cooker all day.

To make the white-bean colcannon, use a stick blender or food processor to purée the beans with the milk until very smooth.

Put the kale and any water that's still clinging to the leaves in a saucepan over medium heat. Stir for about 1–2 minutes until the kale has begun to soften. Add the bean purée and spring onions and stir to heat through and combine, but be careful not to let it catch on the bottom of the pan. If it seems a little dry or begins to catch, add a few tablespoons water or milk. Taste and season with salt and pepper.

Serve the sticky braised beef spooned on top of the white-bean colcannon and top with chopped parsley.

BRAISED CHICKEN WITH WHITE BEANS, MUSTARD AND CIDER

Serves 4

The original iteration of this dish involved rabbit. It went hunting for all the flavours of Normandy and clamped them together in one pot. Its appeal lay in the perfect balance between the tang of the mustard and the sweetness of the apple cider. Yet I know that any recipe that starts with 'joint your rabbit' may cause half of you to turn the page instantly. And so I've altered it for you, but mostly I've done it for my doppelgänger. You see, there's another Tori. We sat next to each other in a slate-grey and Pantone 485 Red office for three years. We were two women in our late twenties, doing exactly the same job, with the same first name in a small team of four. Our birthdays are separated by just a day, we have identical initials, matching freckles on the top of our right ears and a shared, macabre fascination with sharks. Yet, unlike me, Tori has a pet rabbit called Rudy who is one of the great loves of her life. So out of respect for them both I can now happily confirm that this one-pot, slow-carb wonder works just as well with chicken thighs on the bone as it does with a bunny. Phew.

1 tbsp olive oil
6 skinless chicken thighs on the bone
2 rashers of smoked bacon, cut into thin strips
4 large shallots or 2 onions, peeled and cut into
  slim half-moons
1 garlic clove, peeled and thinly sliced
4 sprigs of fresh thyme
8 prunes, pitted
300 ml apple cider
1 x 400-g tin of cannellini or butter beans, rinsed
½ tbsp Dijon mustard
1 tbsp crème fraîche (optional)
sea salt and freshly ground black pepper

Preheat the oven to 180°C/350°F/Gas 4.

Add the olive oil to a flameproof and heatproof casserole dish over medium–high heat and sear the chicken pieces on each side until you have a light golden colour. Remove the chicken pieces and set them aside.

In the same dish, fry the bacon for a minute or so until the fat has rendered and it starts to crisp up. Add the shallots or onions, garlic and a few picked thyme leaves and sauté for 5–7 minutes until the shallots or onions have softened.

Add the browned chicken pieces and prunes to the dish. Pour in the cider and turn up the heat. Bring to the boil and use a spoon to scrape up any flavour that's darkened on the bottom of the dish.

Fold in the beans, mustard and the remaining thyme sprigs. The liquid should come halfway up the chicken pieces, so add a little more water if it doesn't. Clamp the lid on and bake in the preheated oven for 1½–2 hours. The chicken should easily pull off the bone and the sauce be sticky and rich.

Serve the chicken over the onion and bean mixture. Add a teaspoon of crème fraîche if you want things a little richer. Season with salt and pepper to taste.

QUINOA-STUFFED MUSHROOMS

Serves 2

Food is a lovely way of bringing people together; of making us feel included, wanted and respected. Unless it's the festive season and you've committed to serving turkey, bread and sausage stuffing and later find at your table a vegetarian, a gluten-intolerant and a couple who are trying to lay off the white stodge. Oops. This is a dish which can help you avoid that scenario. It's a sort of stuffing, but instead of ducking inside a bird, it sits in the bellies of mushrooms. Quinoa stands in for bread and there are two types of cheese for hearty stickability. Nestled in with it all are all sorts of woodsy champions; rosemary, garlic, a garland of wilted spinach, and for a little sweet tang, dried blueberries. They're also lovely made with small button mushrooms as a canapé, or medium mushrooms as a side dish. Add a splodge of crème fraîche just before serving and they're downright civil and welcoming. And if all else goes astray, know they go very well with a glass of fizz.

2 or more large Portobello mushrooms
   (approximately 250 g in total)
2 tbsp olive oil
2 garlic cloves, peeled and finely diced
2 tsp fresh rosemary leaves, finely chopped
45 g quinoa, cooked in 125 ml water for 15 minutes
   until plumped, or 120 g cooked quinoa
80 g baby spinach, roughly chopped
30 g Parmesan, grated
3 tbsp/60 g Boursin cheese (or soft goats' cheese)
3 tbsp dried blueberries
2 tbsp flaked almonds
2 tbsp pumpkin seeds
crème fraîche and freshly ground black pepper, to serve

Preheat the oven to 180°C/350°F/Gas 4.

Pull the stems out of all the mushrooms, dice them and set them aside. Place the mushrooms, dark belly side up, on a baking tray.

Put the olive oil in a frying pan over medium heat. Add the garlic and rosemary and sauté gently until they start to soften, then add the diced mushroom stems and sauté until soft.

Add the cooked quinoa and the spinach and stir until the spinach wilts. Fold in the cheeses and the dried blueberries. Stir until the cheeses have melted through the quinoa and spinach. Spoon the mixture into the dark bellies of the mushrooms. Scatter the tops with the almonds and pumpkin seeds.

Bake the mushrooms in the preheated oven for about 25 minutes, or until they are cooked and the almonds are toasted. Serve with a splodge of crème fraîche and some black pepper.

TIP: *If you can't find dried blueberries, substitute with dried cranberries or currants. Similarly, if pumpkin seeds prove a stretch, just use more flaked almonds or add some pine nuts. These mushrooms can be prepared ahead of time and left in the fridge on a baking tray covered in clingfilm. Just remove the clingfilm and bake when wanted.*

Once upon a time, for me dessert was all about glorious
heft. There was nothing more satisfying than the podge
of a pudding. Bread and butter, summer berry, sticky
toffee and lemon delicious were my most beloved.
It took a lot to stop me from going back for seconds
of each of them. These days I've found satisfaction
and delight in sweets that take a brighter, lighter tack.
Whether it's fresh stone fruits in an almond-based
clafoutis, or the spiced warmth of cinnamon-poached
pears or a rhubarb crumble with a slow-carb topping,
these are the flavours which now bring me the greatest
joy. I love these desserts because the majority of them
work just as well for me as they do for my gluten-
intolerant friends. I love them because most of them
are a breeze to make (there need only be three
ingredients in the chocolate mousse and the batter for
the loaf cakes can be made in a blender in four minutes).
And I love them because of how they make me feel. Sure
there's some sugar here and the occasional indulgence
of chocolate (The Hungry One would hazard that a life
without chocolate is not much of a life at all).

   I'm not suggesting that the leanest version of you
will be eating dessert every night. But when Saturday
night or a celebration rolls around, these are the
recipes I reach for. And these are the ones which
have me scraping my plate for every last taste.

MOREISH
PUDDINGS

LATTE CUSTARDS AND CHOCOLATE HAZELNUT CHEWS

Makes 4 custards and 16–18 chews

My husband, The Hungry One, is a man with clear tastes and preferences. He likes chocolate. He loves coffee – perhaps a little too much. But curiously, top of all things, he values texture in his food. And when it comes to a cookie, it's the chew which is key. These choc-hazelnut biscuits are the ultimate cookie to him: they're intensely flavoured with cocoa and pull lightly at your teeth. They're also somewhat magical in their make up – there are no flour, butter or raising agents to contend with, just egg whites, cocoa and icing sugar. A few nuts for bite and a little sprinkle of salt will really help them stand out. What they call for on the side is something silken to dunk them into. If you're entertaining, these latte custards can be prepared ahead of time and left to rest in the fridge. They're an absolute doddle to make. And best of all, they'll make use of the egg yolks you've got left over from your cookies. Which is a good thing, since one of the only things The Hungry One doesn't like is waste.

Chocolate hazelnut chews

4 egg whites
3 pinches of salt
100 g cocoa powder
280 g icing sugar
155 g blanched hazelnuts, roughly chopped
    (reserve a few whole hazelnuts to decorate, if you like)

Latte custards

300 ml milk
2 shots (60 ml) of espresso or 2 tbsp strong filter coffee
    (you can use decaf if you prefer)
4 egg yolks
1 whole egg
110 g caster sugar
20 g dark chocolate, grated

Equipment

baking tray lined with baking paper
4 ramekins, 200-ml capacity, greased

To make the chocolate hazelnut chews, preheat the oven to 180°C/350°F/Gas 4.

In a very clean bowl and using an electric whisk on medium speed, whisk the egg whites and a pinch of the salt for 2 minutes, or until the eggs are foaming. Gently rain in the cocoa powder and icing sugar and beat for another 2–3 minutes until you have a glossy, well-incorporated mixture that stands up in peaks. Gently fold in the chopped hazelnuts.

Use a tablespoon to portion and transfer the mixture in mounds onto the lined baking tray, leaving 2–3 cm between the cookies to allow them to spread while baking. Decorate with whole hazelnuts, if you like. Sprinkle the remaining salt over the tops of the cookies. Bake them in the preheated oven for 20 minutes, or until cracks appear on the tops of cookies and you can peel them off the baking tray. If they stick to the base, return them to the oven for a few more minutes. Transfer them to a wire rack to cool while you make the latte custards.

Reduce the oven temperature to 160°C/325°F/Gas 3 and put the prepared ramekins in a roasting dish.

Put the milk and espresso in a small saucepan over low heat and bring to a simmer.

In a bowl, whisk together the egg yolks, whole egg and sugar until the sugar has dissolved and the mixture is pale. Add one-quarter of a cup of the simmered latte to the bowl and mix well, then gradually add the rest of the latte in a gentle stream. Try not to make it too foamy.

Pour the latte custard into a jug through a sieve and try to skim off any foam on the top. Now pour it into the ramekins. Boil some water in the kettle and transfer the dish or ramekins to the oven, leaving the oven door open. Pour the boiling water into the roasting dish until it comes halfway up the sides of the ramekins.

Bake the custards in the oven for 45 minutes, or until they just wobble in the centre when you shuffle them. Chill for 1 hour or so, or until ready to serve. Serve with grated chocolate on top and the chocolate hazelnut chews on the side for dunking.

CLEMENTINE TARTA DE SANTIAGO

Serves 6–8

I first tasted Tarta de Santiago ('cake of St James') in the back streets of Madrid, but it was at London's Borough Market that I really fell for its charms. There are few finer ways to spend an hour on a Thursday afternoon than with a flat white from Monmouth or Elliot's and a sliver of flourless almond cake from beneath the glass canister on the counter of the Brindisa store. I'd often find myself still licking cinnamon and icing sugar from my fingertips while looking out across the Thames to St Pauls – and occasionally pinching myself. Life can sometimes be very sweet. An authentic Tarta de Santiago is flavoured with orange, though I find the genial twinkle of clementine works just as well. A pile of poached clementine segments are just the thing to place in the centre of the cake prior to serving. Meanwhile, the syrup makes an excellent sticky drizzle (and any left over is a real treat as a base for a cocktail – try shaking a dribble of it with gin and Campari over ice).

5 eggs
220 g caster sugar
250 g ground almonds
grated zest of 1 clementine or mandarin
½ tsp ground cinnamon

Poached clementines
6 clementines
250 g caster sugar
600 ml water

To serve
icing sugar, for dusting
25 g roughly chopped almonds
Greek yoghurt

Equipment
23-cm springform cake tin, greased and lined with
   baking paper

To poach the clementines, wash them and then prick them with a fork at the top, the bottom and 5 times around the circumference of the fruit.

Take a saucepan large enough to hold the clementines. Put the sugar and water in the pan over low heat and stir until the sugar has dissolved. Add the clementines and simmer, uncovered, for 30–45 minutes, rotating them occasionally until the skins are very soft and a fork easily slides in. Allow the clementines to cool in the syrup until they are cool enough to handle.

Slip the fruit from the skins and remove any obvious pips. Place the segments in a bowl and return the skins to the sugar syrup. Simmer the syrup for another 20 minutes until it has reduced by half. Now you can either chop the skins into slivers and disperse them through the syrup, or discard them.

Preheat the oven to 180°C/350°F/Gas 4.

Put the eggs and sugar in a bowl and use an electric whisk to beat them until thick and pale. Fold in the ground almonds, fresh clementine or mandarin zest and cinnamon.

Transfer the mixture to the prepared cake tin and bake in the preheated oven for 40–45 minutes or until a skewer inserted in the middle comes out clean. Set the tin on a wire rack for 10 minutes before removing the cake from the tin.

Serve the cake warm and dusted with icing sugar, with the poached clementine segments, warm syrup, chopped almonds and some Greek yoghurt.

TIP: *Beyond clementines, you could also tweak the recipe by using lemon, lime or orange zest. Or triple the quantity of cinnamon and add some ground ginger and allspice for a Christmassy twist.*

YOGHURT PANNA COTTAS WITH CINNAMON-POACHED PEARS

Serves 4

These cinnamon-braised pears are as romantic as an afternoon stroll over brittle amber leaves. All they cry out for is a cool and elegant companion. Rather than the heft of cream, the lactic tang of yoghurt makes these panna cottas a considerate dessert for everyone, particularly since they're easily made earlier in the day and forgotten about until just before serving. When it comes to the pears, you'll probably find firm-textured fruit will poach better, drinking in the flavoured syrup while maintaining their arched shape even after a spell in the pot. For anyone worried about extricating the panna cottas from their moulds, here's a trick: if you swipe the inside of your plastic cups with a little neutral oil before pouring the mix in, when set they should easily shirk away from the edge before slinking onto the plate. Alternatively, you could set the panna cottas in small bowls and serve them with the fruit and syrup forming a shallow chestnut pool on top.

Yoghurt panna cottas
200 ml pouring cream
50 g caster sugar
2 gold-strength gelatine leaves
275 g Greek yoghurt
1 tsp neutral-tasting oil

Cinnamon pears
1 litre water
220 g muscovado sugar
2 cinnamon sticks
4 Beurré Bosc or Kaiser pears, peeled, cored and quartered
4 tbsp walnuts, roughly chopped

Equipment
4 plastic cups or shallow bowls

Begin the panna cottas at least 4 hours before you want to serve them. Put the cream and sugar in a saucepan over low heat and bring it to a simmer, stirring until the sugar has dissolved.

Meanwhile, submerge the gelatine leaves in a bowl of cold water for a few minutes until they become pliable and slippery.

Squeeze the soaked gelatine leaves well and add them to the warm cream. Whisk with a balloon whisk until the gelatine has dissolved. Add the yoghurt and whisk gently until smooth.

Swipe the insides of plastic cups with the oil on some kitchen paper. If you are serving the panna cottas in shallow bowls, there's no need to oil them. Pour the panna cotta mixture into the cups and refrigerate for 4 hours or overnight to set.

To make the cinnamon pears, take a saucepan large enough to hold the pears. Put the water, sugar and cinnamon sticks in the pan over medium heat. Bring it to a simmer and allow the sugar to dissolve.

Meanwhile, cut out a circle of baking paper the same size as the pan, and then cut a small hole out of the middle. This is your cartouche. Add the pears to the pan and cover with the cartouche. Simmer (without the lid) at a gentle blip for 15–25 minutes until the point of a knife easily slides into the pears. Pluck the pears from the liquid and boil the syrup over high heat until it has reduced by half.

Just before you are ready to serve, use your index finger to pull the set panna cottas away from the edge of the cup – this will allow air in and break the seal. Place a plate over the mouth of the cup, flip them both over and allow the panna cotta to slink down onto the plate. Serve with the pears, a drizzle of syrup and the walnuts over the top.

<u>TIP:</u> *Please bear in mind that using a cartouche with the centre cleaved out for poaching the pears may seem like extra work, but it's worth it: it helps ensure that all of the pears remain submerged in the syrup, giving you more consistent texture across the fruit.*

CHIA, MANGO, COCONUT AND MACADAMIA TRIFLE

Serves 4

If there's a taste of a Sydney summer, it's probably an errant drip from a ripe mango as it traces from your pinky down to your elbow. Often while chasing it you'll collect the faint smell of coconut-scented sunscreen. If, like me, every now and again you miss that taste so badly it hurts, this dessert may help. Layered in glasses, it uses plump orbs of chia in place of custard or cake. Lychees and macadamia nuts add some more textural interest, but the real hero is the mango. Of course this is best when made with spanking-fresh fruit – but here's a secret. This dessert is also something to keep in your back pocket when you're stuck inside on a grey day with only tins and packets at your disposal. Take a tin of sliced mango, a tin of coconut milk and a tin of lychees. Drain, blend, mix and serve. It's just a trifling effort for a terrific dessert. Note: this also works well as part of a brunch or breakfast spread.

70 g chia seeds
400 ml coconut milk
1 x 425-g tin of mango pieces, drained,
  or 2 medium mangos, peeled and pitted
1 x 425-g tin of lychees, drained,
  or 20 lychees, shelled and pitted
2 tbsp macadamia nuts, roughly chopped

Whisk together the chia seeds and coconut milk.

Using a stick blender or food processor, blitz three-quarters of the tinned or fresh mango until you have a smooth purée. Slice the remaining mango into slivers and cut the lychees in half and set them aside.

Swirl the mango purée through the chia-coconut mixture and divide half the mixture between 4 glasses.

Add a layer of sliced mango and lychee halves. Top with the mango-chia-coconut mixture and place in the fridge for 2 hours or overnight to set. Top with the remaining sliced mango and lychee halves and the macadamias just before serving.

TUTTI FRUTTI CLAFOUTIS

Serves 4

A clafoutis' genus lies somewhere between a pancake and a puffed fruit pudding. A French dessert, it is classically made with cherries still carrying their pits in their bellies. The pits gift an almond twinge to the batter but also mean it can be wise to have a dentist on speed-dial while serving it. While cherries are gorgeous, to me the potential rhyming novelty of serving a tutti frutti clafoutis is way too good to pass up. Reach for as wide a bounty of stone fruits as you dare; pitted nectarines, peaches, apricots, cherries and plums are all wicked inclusions. Either make it in four petite pans, or serve as slices with vanilla ice cream pooling over the top. While this is an easy dessert to pull together for a small group, it is also lovely for brunch. It's best hot, but there's no reason why you can't eat the leftovers cold the next day with yoghurt.

80 g ground almonds
2 tbsp cornflour
4 tbsp caster sugar
250 ml whole milk
2 eggs, lightly beaten
2 egg yolks
600 g mixed stone fruits, eg plums, peaches, nectarines,
  apricots, cherries
20 g unsalted butter
handful of flaked almonds
ice cream or yoghurt, to serve (optional)

Equipment
23-cm non-stick frying pan with a heatproof handle,
  or 23-cm round baking dish

Preheat the oven to 200°C/400°F/Gas 6.

Whisk the ground almonds, cornflour and half the sugar into the milk, beaten eggs, and egg yolks until you have a smooth batter.

Pit and slice the fruit into halves or chunks if they're large peaches or nectarines. Place them in the frying pan or baking dish, dot them with dabs of the butter and scatter the remaining sugar over the top. Bake in the preheated oven for 10 minutes to soften. Remove the pan from the oven and leave the oven on.

Pour the batter over the baked fruit, scatter the flaked almonds over the top and bake in the oven for 20 minutes, or until the clafoutis has puffed up and the almonds are toasted.

Eat the clafoutis warm, with ice cream – or cold, for breakfast, with yoghurt.

PEANUT BUTTER AND JAM PUDDINGS

Makes 12 small puddings, or serves 6 (most people will probably find it hard to eat just one)

For the longest time, I never understood the appeal of combining peanut butter with jelly or jam. It was the stickiness of it all that upset me. That was until I twigged that combining a touch of salt with the sweet is one of the great secrets of the universe. It pulls everything into balance – and it's exactly what's at work here. If you like, an extra sprinkling of salt on the top of these deceptively light puddings manages to amplify the sweetness of the berries hiding inside. Serve them with a dollop of jam and some roasted peanuts on the top for crunch. And perhaps a little cream or ice cream on the side.

4 eggs
260 g chunky peanut butter
115 g caster sugar
1 tsp sea salt flakes
60 ml vegetable oil
½ tsp bicarbonate of soda
½ tsp baking powder
125 ml milk
70 g fresh or frozen raspberries

To serve
¼ cup raspberry jam, warmed with a small splash of water
2 tbsp roasted peanuts
vanilla ice cream

Equipment
12-hole muffin tin, greased and dusted with flour

Preheat the oven to 180°C/350°F/Gas 4.

In a bowl, whisk together all the ingredients, except the raspberries, until they are well combined and smooth. Divide the mixture between the holes of the muffin tin.

Divide the raspberries between the puddings, gently prodding them into their middles.

Bake the puddings in the preheated oven for about 20 minutes, or until they are golden and puffed and a skewer inserted in the middle comes out clean (but for a bit of raspberry smear).

Allow to cool in the muffin tin for 5 minutes, then carefully remove each pudding. Serve with a drizzling of the jam-syrup, the peanuts, and some vanilla ice cream.

SALZBURGER NOCKERL, OR BERRIES AND CLOUDS

Serves 4

There are only 150,000 people who live in Salzburg. Yet every year more than 300,000 Sound of Music devotees will make a pilgrimage to the city. Sure they might be interested in seeing Mozart's birthplace. Others might want to dine at arguably the oldest restaurant in Europe (circa 803), drink at the Stiegl brewery and wander by a blue river on a clear day. But really, most have come to enjoy tea with jam and bread, crisp apple strudel and schnitzel with noodles. Once you've sung do-re-mi enough and clamoured out of your carb hole, if you haven't gone into complete sugar shock (from the food and the film), there's always the option of Salzburger Nockerl for dessert. This local speciality involves berries (traditionally raspberries, but in deference to the von Trapps' berry-picking escapades I've opted for blueberries) topped with buoyant clouds of souffléed meringue. The meringues are classically formed into three peaks to resemble the hills bordering the city. It's a dessert best served warm with some custard on the side. And afterwards, there's no need for you to climb every mountain, but a hike up at least one small hill will help slake some of the indulgence.

450 g blueberries (defrosted and drained if frozen)
grated zest and juice of ½ lemon
50 g icing sugar, plus extra for dusting
7 eggs, separated
a pinch of salt
70 g caster sugar
1½ tbsp cornflour
custard, to serve (optional)

Equipment
20-cm square baking dish, greased

Preheat the oven to 180°C/350°F/Gas 4.

Put the berries, lemon zest and juice in the prepared baking dish and sprinkle with the icing sugar.

If you have an electric whisk, now is the time to use it. Put the egg whites and salt in a very clean bowl and whisk until the eggs are foamy. Add 50 g of the caster sugar, a tablespoon at a time, and whisk well between each addition. Keep whisking until the whites have quadrupled in size and are stiff enough to hold their shape when you hold the bowl upside down (over your head, if you're brave enough).

Put the egg yolks and the remaining sugar in a separate bowl and whisk until the eggs are fluffy. Beat in the cornflour until incorporated. Finally, carefully fold the mixture into the beaten egg whites with a metal spoon, in 3 stages, trying to maintain as much air in the mixture as possible.

Portion the mixture over the berries in 3 mounds to resemble the 3 mountains that surround Salzburg.

Bake the pudding in the preheated oven for 30 minutes, or until a light crust has formed on the outside and the interior of the egg topping is no longer liquidy – a skewer inserted in the middle of the topping should come out clean. Turn the oven off and leave the pudding inside with the door closed for a further 15 minutes before removing it and serving it immediately. Dust with icing sugar and serve with a little custard, if you like.

PASSIONFRUIT AND RASPBERRY NOUGAT PARFAIT

Serves 8

This parfait carries me straight to an Australian Christmas, when the air is muggy and your hair is still soggy from the last dip in the swimming pool. My mother would always make a version of this, studded with berries and decked with toasted nuts to be sliced as the last taste in our Christmas Eve holiday meal. To this day, the original recipe remains scrawled on three scraps of paper and spends 50 weeks of the year lying in a drawer in her house, along with gold wrapping paper and spools of red ribbon. My take is a little sunnier, rippling the sparkle of passionfruit curd through the cooled ricotta and whipped cream. While you could weave all of the curd through the dessert, I like to keep some of it aside, either to drape over the top of the pudding, or to swirl through yoghurt the next day. Christmas breakfast has rarely tasted so good.

Passionfruit curd
4 egg yolks
115 g caster sugar
100 ml lemon juice
grated zest of 1 lemon
pulp scooped out of 2 passionfruit
60 g unsalted butter

Parfait
400 g ricotta
165 g caster sugar
300 ml whipping cream
100 g nougat, chopped
100 g fresh or frozen raspberries
¾ cup cooled Passionfruit Curd (see below)

Equipment
20 x 12.5-cm loaf tin, base and sides double-lined with baking paper

For the passionfruit curd, whisk together the egg yolks and sugar until they are fluffy. Transfer to a saucepan with the remaining ingredients and set over medium–low heat. Stir until the mixture thickens like mayonnaise. If it is lumpy, strain it before pouring it into jars to cool.

For the parfait, blend the ricotta and sugar until smooth. In a separate bowl, whisk the cream until soft peaks form. Fold all the ingredients together, then swirl through them three-quarters of a cup of the passionfruit curd until you have a ripple effect.

Spoon the mixture into the prepared loaf tin and freeze it for 6–8 hours. To serve, turn the parfait out of the tin, slice it and arrange the slices on a platter. Put the slices in the fridge for 30 minutes before serving to allow them to soften to the right consistency. Dollop any remaining passionfruit curd over the top of the slices.

TIP: *This must be made at least 6 hours before serving. It benefits from softening in the fridge for 15–20 minutes before cutting.*

BAKED RICOTTA-STUFFED PEACHES

Serves 2 as a modest, light dessert (but if you want a more robust serving, scale up as needed)

There are dishes in a repertoire that are inspired by a place, igniting memories of wonderful times away. And then there are others which act more as Post-it notes; an edible reminder to yourself that one day, you will make it there. For me, the place is the Amalfi coast, and the dish is this. Every time I roast sweet peaches, plumping their bellies with nutmeg-spiced ricotta first, I imagine myself strolling the steep streets of Positano. I may be eating this in my pyjamas at home, but after two bites of this I'm gone.

1 large (or 2 medium) peach, halved and pitted
3 tbsp ricotta
1 tbsp muscovado sugar
½ tsp ground cinnamon
½ tsp grated nutmeg
1 tbsp chopped pistachios
honey and Greek yoghurt or crème fraîche, to serve (optional)

Preheat the oven to 180°C/350°F/Gas 4.

Use a melon baller to hollow out the peach a little further, where the pit was. Place the peach halves, cut side up, in individual ramekins or snuggled up to one another in a baking dish.

Mix together the ricotta, sugar and spices. Transfer the mix into the bellies of the peaches. Bake the peaches in the preheated oven for 15–20 minutes until the ricotta has bronzed and the peaches have softened.

Serve the peaches either warm or at room temperature, topped with the pistachios and drizzled with honey. Some Greek yoghurt or crème fraîche on the side would also be a nice addition.

CHOCOLATE, BLACK BEAN AND CHERRY CAKE

Makes 8–10 slices

I've become a little evangelical about these cakes. Why? For one, they're the simplest cakes I've ever encountered. You have a blender or a food processor? You have a loaf tin? You have an oven? Done. There's no flour, so they're perfect for your gluten-intolerant friends. And together they form two sides of one joyous coin. The first is dark with chocolate and will satisfy even the most insane hormonal craving. The second is angelic with rose water, almonds and raspberries. These are both my go-to, emergency cakes, taking turns week on week. They're smart enough to be served warm with crème fraîche or double cream. They're sturdy enough for lunch boxes. They're not so evil that you couldn't justify a slice at 3pm with a cup of tea after you've tottered to the post office. I don't want to get too crazy here, but there's every chance that these cakes may change your life.

1 x 400-g tin of black beans, rinsed
3 eggs
100 g caster sugar
1 shot (30 ml) of espresso or 1 tbsp strong filter coffee (you can use decaf if you prefer)
3 tbsp cocoa powder
1 tsp baking powder (check it is gluten-free if cooking for a coeliac crowd)
125 g cherries, pitted (can be frozen, and you can also substitute other berries), plus extra to serve
icing sugar, yoghurt, crème fraîche or fresh cherries, to serve (optional)

Equipment
20 x 12.5-cm loaf tin, greased and lined with baking paper

Preheat the oven to 180°C/350°F/Gas 4.

Using a stick blender and mixing bowl, blender or food processor, combine all the ingredients except the cherries and blitz until smooth. The batter will appear quite liquidy but don't worry. Pour the batter into the prepared loaf tin and scatter the cherries over the top.

Bake the loaf in the preheated oven for 35 minutes, or until a skewer inserted in the middle comes out with a few fudgy crumbs on it.

Leave to cool in the tin for 5 minutes, then turn it out. Dust with icing sugar and serve warm with more cherries, yoghurt or crème fraîche for dessert, or allow it to cool and enjoy it with a cup of tea.

RASPBERRY, WHITE BEAN AND ROSE CAKE

Makes 8–10 slices

1 x 400-g tin of cannellini beans, rinsed
3 eggs
100 g caster sugar
1 tbsp rosewater
3 tbsp ground almonds
1 tsp baking powder (check it is gluten-free if cooking for a coeliac crowd)
125 g raspberries (can be frozen, and you can also substitute other berries, or pitted cherries), plus extra to serve
icing sugar, yoghurt or crème fraîche, to serve (optional)

Equipment
20 x 12.5-cm loaf tin, greased and lined with baking paper

Preheat the oven to 180°C/350°F/Gas 4.

Using a stick blender and mixing bowl, blender or food processor, combine all the ingredients except the raspberries and blitz until smooth. The batter will appear quite liquidy but don't worry. Pour the batter into the prepared loaf tin and scatter the raspberries over the top.

Bake the loaf in the preheated oven for 35 minutes, or until a skewer inserted in the middle comes out with a few fudgy crumbs on it.

Leave to cool in the tin for 5 minutes, then turn it out. Dust with icing sugar and serve warm with more raspberries, yoghurt or crème fraîche for dessert, or allow it to cool and enjoy it with a cup of tea.

RHUBARB, APPLE AND BERRY SLOW CRUMBLE

Serves 4

The boundaries between a crumble, a crisp, a buckle and a slump are blurry. All seem to involve poached or baked fruit and a topping usually melding sugar, butter and a grain. When it comes to my pudding I'm less interested in definitional purity and more intrigued by having something that tastes terrific. The golden thing about this crumble isn't just the way that the tartness of the rhubarb is mellowed by segments of apple and oozing berries. Nor is it the wink of spice in the cinnamon or ginger, or the crunch from the flaked almonds and toasted oats. It's the other bits that make you feel good: the ground flaxseed and the sneaky smashed banana. An over-ripe banana mushed into the topping helps pull down the quantity of raw sugar and contributes both a delicious caramel–sweetness and a rustic chew to the topping. This may be categorised as a 'slow crumble', but in our house, it never lasts long. Once again, while this is a delicious dessert, it's also worth considering as a celebratory brunch or breakfast option, with Greek yoghurt instead of ice cream.

100 g unsalted butter, chilled and cubed,
   plus 30 g for the fruit
90 g rolled oats
50 g ground flaxseed/linseed
75 g flaked almonds
25 g muscovado sugar
1 ripe banana, mashed
2 tsp ground ginger
2 tsp ground cinnamon
5 sticks (250 g) of rhubarb, cut into 4-cm batons
4 Pink Lady apples, peeled, cored and cut into eighths
125 g blackberries
Greek yoghurt, crème fraîche, double cream or ice cream,
   to serve

Equipment
large, shallow baking dish, greased

Preheat the oven 180°C/350°F/Gas 4.

To make a crumble topping, put the 100 g butter, oats, flaxseed/linseed, almonds, sugar, banana, ginger and cinnamon in a bowl. Use your fingers to mash everything together into a rustic tumble. It should be rough and lumpy. Refrigerate the topping until ready to bake.

Put the rhubarb and apple and half the blackberries in a saucepan with the 30 g butter and cook over medium heat for 10–15 minutes until the rhubarb and apple have begun to soften.

Transfer the softened fruit to the prepared baking dish and dot with the remaining berries.

Scatter the crumble topping over the fruit, ensuring there are lots of craggy edges.

Bake the crumble in the preheated oven for 30 minutes, or until the top is bronzed and crisp. Serve hot with Greek yoghurt, crème fraîche, double cream or ice cream. Or enjoy cold, for breakfast.

PEPPERMINT CHOCOLATE MOUSSE WITH PISTACHIOS

Serves 2, but can easily be scaled up as needed

It's hard not to love a three-ingredient mousse. All that's required is a hot cup of tea, a few chunks of dark chocolate and some egg whites. This recipe had a Goldilocks start in life. Two egg whites were too flat. Four muffled the taste of the chocolate. But three were just right. While this version uses peppermint tea, recalling the retro tastes of my parents' mint 'After Eight' chocolates which were reserved for occasional dinner parties, you could easily recruit other flavours. Earl or Lady Grey tea would contribute some pleasing aromas, ginger tea would be a refreshing change or a long black coffee would give it a little extra get-up-and-go. Experiment to your heart's content. Something to bear in mind: this is a mousse that is even better the next day, making it the perfect thing to quickly prepare on a Thursday night if you have people coming over after work on a Friday.

1 peppermint tea bag
100 ml boiling water
125 g dark chocolate, chopped
3 egg whites
a pinch of salt
8 fresh mint leaves
2 tsp pistachio nuts, toasted and chopped

Equipment
2 x 200-ml ramekins

Steep the peppermint tea bag in the boiling water until the water is cool enough for you to hold your finger in it for 5 seconds. Remove the tea bag and discard it.

Put 100 g of the chocolate and the peppermint tea in a small saucepan over low heat. Stir until two-thirds of the chocolate has melted, then take the pan off the heat.

Add the remaining chocolate to the pan and stir it, off the heat, until it has melted. This will help temper the chocolate a little, making it glossier and preventing it from becoming grainy.

Transfer the melted mint chocolate to a bowl and stir until it is smooth and has come to room temperature. Add the egg whites and salt and beat with an electric whisk for 4–6 minutes until ribbons form in the mixture.

Pour into the ramekins and refrigerate for 4–6 hours or overnight.

Serve the mousses topped with the mint leaves and chopped pistachios.

ORANGE, CHOCOLATE AND HAZELNUT PUDDINGS

Serves 4

If there are three desserts which sum up the 90s to me it would be tiramisù, sticky date pudding and soft-centred chocolate puddings. Granted, there were lots of things about that decade which might best be forgotten (combat boots, wallet chains and platform sandals included), but an oozing fondant isn't one of them. This example uses ground hazelnuts for flour, which also contributes a slight Nutella flavour, while the orange zest contributes a bit of a twist. If you fancy a pronounced 'jaffa' flavour in your dessert feel free to use the zest of a whole orange rather than half. These are a great pudding for entertaining, as you can easily prepare the batter in the afternoon and bake to order while the main course is being served; but don't delay in getting them to the table, as the residual heat in the puddings will keep cooking them all the way through. There may be lots of things which have gone out of style, but the molten centre of a chocolate pudding is one taste which will never date.

110 g caster sugar, plus 1 tbsp for dusting
60 g unsalted butter
1 shot (30 ml) of espresso
100 g dark chocolate (minimum 70% cocoa solids), chopped
2 eggs
grated zest of 1 orange
100 g ground hazelnuts

To serve
ice cream, Greek yoghurt or crème fraîche

Equipment
4 x 200-ml ramekins, greased

Preheat the oven to 220°C/425°F/Gas 7.

Sprinkle the 1 tbsp caster sugar inside a greased ramekin, rolling it around to ensure the sides are evenly covered, then pour the excess sugar into the next ramekin and repeat until they have all been dusted.

Put the butter, espresso and chocolate in a saucepan over medium heat and stir until melted and smooth. Alternatively, use a microwave.

Put the eggs and 110 g sugar in a bowl and beat with an electric whisk for 2–3 minutes until pale and fluffy. Pour the mixture into the melted chocolate, stir, then fold in half the orange zest and all the ground hazelnuts.

Divide the mixture between the prepared ramekins (about 4 tablespoons each). Put the ramekins on a baking tray and bake the puddings in the preheated oven for 15 minutes, or until firm to the touch and still slightly molten in the centre.

Serve the puddings hot with the remaining orange zest, ice cream, Greek yoghurt or crème fraîche pooling on the crest of each one. If you really wanted to push the boat out, you could swirl some good-quality marmalade with softened vanilla ice cream and re-freeze it, then and add a scoop of that on the side (or use some of the syrup from the poached clementines on page 150).

INDEX

A

adzuki beans 10, 11
  miso aubergine with ginger tofu
    and adzuki beans 139
aïoli, red-eye 42
ajo blanco with red grapes 60
ajvar, lentil 'meatballs' with tomato and
  133
all the nanas' chicken, lemon, egg and
  white bean soup 48
almonds: ajo blanco with red grapes 60
  almond blueberry pancakes 14
  clementine tarta de Santiago 150
  five-spice soy roasted almonds 36
apple cider vinegar 10
apples: green soup 62
  rhubarb, apple and berry slow
    crumble 167
  savoury baked apples with goats' curd
    and Parma ham 70
  sort-of-Waldorf salad 101
apricots: chia and apricot quinoa
  porridge 23
artichokes: artichokes with red-eye
  aïoli 42
  cannellini bean, Parmesan and
    artichoke dip 34
asparagus dippers, gooey eggs with 16
aubergines: aubergine 'parm' 127
  miso aubergine with ginger tofu
    and adzuki beans 139
  smokey aubergine with tomatoes,
    pickled onion, parsley and
    pomegranate molasses 79
avocados: guacamole 26
  prawn, avocado and edamame salad
    106

B

bacon: pigs in kimchee blankets 39
  prawn and quinoa grits 136
  smoked paprika chia frittatas 19
  soft eggs with smokey baked beans
    25
bananas: rhubarb, apple and berry
  slow crumble 167
basil pesto 75
beans 10–11
beef: baked white-bean gnocchi with
  meatballs 122

pork, beef and mushroom-stuffed
  cabbage rolls 130
  sticky braised beef 142
beetroot: duck breasts with roast
  beetroot, radish and cocoa 140
  roast beetroot and carrots with ras el
    hanout, mint and labneh 80
berries and clouds 158
Bircher muesli, chia 22
black beans 10, 11
  black bean, chorizo, sweet potato and
    coconut bowl 82
  chocolate, black bean and cherry cake
    164
  griddled chillies stuffed with feta,
    black beans and pumpkin seeds 104
  Mexican baked eggs 26
  piri piri chicken with black beans and
    tomatoes 116
Black Forest slow granola parfaits 30
blackberries: rhubarb, apple and berry
  slow crumble 167
Bloody Mary tomato soup 54
blue cheese soufflés 120
blueberries: almond blueberry pancakes
  14
  Salzburger nockerl 158
borlotti beans 10, 11
  borlotti beans with roasted pear,
    walnuts and blue cheese 87
  soft eggs with smokey baked beans
    25
  'three beans' with basil pesto 75
Brazil nuts, broccoli steaks with
  chimichurri and 68
broad bean, fennel, mint, lemon and
  Parmesan salad 100
broccoli: broccoli steaks with
  chimichurri and Brazil nuts 68
  cauliflower and broccoli gratin 73
  green soup 62
brown rice tea salt, edamame with 38
Brussels sprouts with hazelnuts, lentils
  and mustard dressing 72
burgers, Moroccan lamb and chickpea
  111
burnt butter 80
butter beans: baked white-bean
  gnocchi 122
  soft eggs with smokey baked beans 25

C

cabbage rolls, pork, beef and
  mushroom-stuffed 130
cakes: chocolate, black bean and cherry
  cake 164
  raspberry, white bean and rose cake
    164
cannellini beans 10, 11
  ajo blanco with red grapes 60
  braised chicken with white beans,
    mustard and cider 144
  cannellini bean, Parmesan and
    artichoke dip 34
  Mediterranean squid stuffed with
    white bean purée and olives 112
  raspberry, white bean and rose cake
    164
  ribollita 53
  sausages with leeks, caramelised
    onions, mushrooms and beans
    138
  'three beans' with basil pesto 75
  white sauce 127
carrots: carrot purée 67
  roast beetroot and carrots with
    ras el hanout, mint and labneh 80
cauliflower: cauliflower and broccoli
  gratin 73
  cauliflower 'couscous' 76
  cauliflower purée 66
chana dal 11
  dal 78
cheese: aubergine 'parm' 127
  baked white-bean gnocchi with
    meatballs, mozzarella and tomato
    122
  blue cheese soufflés 120
  borlotti beans with roasted pear,
    walnuts and blue cheese 87
  cauliflower and broccoli gratin 73
  feta, mint, lentil and pistachio
    omelettes 20
  griddled chillies stuffed with feta,
    black beans and pumpkin seeds 104
  mushroom and goats' curd 'toasties'
    16
  roasted and fresh tomato skewers
    with mint and halloumi 40
  savoury baked apples with goats' curd
    and Parma ham 70

socca with smoked salmon and whipped curds 28

see also ricotta

cherries: Black Forest slow granola parfaits 30

chocolate, black bean and cherry cake 164

chia seeds 9

chia and apricot quinoa porridge 23

chia Bircher muesli 22

chia, mango, coconut and macadamia trifle 155

peppers stuffed with chia, hummus and pine nuts 98

smoked paprika chia frittatas 19

chicken: all the nanas' chicken, lemon, egg and white bean soup 48

braised chicken with white beans, mustard and cider 144

chicken san choi bow 96

piri piri chicken with black beans and tomatoes 116

quinoa aguadito (Peruvian chicken and coriander soup) 58

sort-of-Waldorf salad 101

thyme-roasted chicken legs 134

chickpea flour/gram/besan 10

socca with smoked salmon and whipped curds 28

chickpeas 10

chickpeas, leek, apple and pear salad 75

chilled curried chickpea soup 57

kale caesar 84

lamb shank and fig tagine 128

Moroccan lamb and chickpea burgers 111

spiced chickpea bombs 44

chillies: griddled chillies stuffed with feta, black beans and pumpkin seeds 104

Mexican baked eggs 26

piri piri marinade 116

yellow split peas with burnt butter and orange 80

chimichurri, broccoli steaks with Brazil nuts and 68

chocolate: chocolate, black bean and cherry cake 164

chocolate hazelnut chews 148

duck breasts with roast beetroot, radish and cocoa 140

orange, chocolate and hazelnut puddings 170

peppermint chocolate mousse with pistachios 168

chorizo: black bean, chorizo, sweet potato and coconut bowl 82

green soup with chorizo almond crumbs 62

choucroute 124

cinnamon coffee protein shakes 14

cinnamon-poached pears 152

clafoutis, tutti frutti 155

clementine tarta de Santiago 150

coconut milk: chia, mango, coconut and macadamia trifle 155

coffee: chocolate, black bean and cherry cake 164

cinnamon coffee protein shakes 14

latte custards 148

colcannon, white-bean 142

cookies: chocolate hazelnut chews 148

coriander: quinoa aguadito (Peruvian chicken and coriander soup) 58

courgettes: courgettes frites 44

quinoa and courgette fritters 40

seabass swaddled in courgette ribbons 90

cream: passionfruit and raspberry nougat parfait 161

yoghurt panna cottas 152

crudités 34

crumble: rhubarb, apple and berry slow crumble 167

cucumber: chilled white bean, cucumber, mint and yoghurt soup 56

raita 108

curried chickpea soup 57

custards, latte 148

D

dal 78

dip, cannellini bean, Parmesan and artichoke 34

duck breasts with roast beetroot, radish and cocoa 140

E

edamame beans: edamame with brown rice tea salt 38

prawn, avocado and edamame salad 106

eggs: feta, mint, lentil and pistachio omelettes 20

gooey eggs with asparagus dippers 16

Mexican baked eggs 26

smoked paprika chia frittatas 19

soft eggs with smokey baked beans 25

F

fennel: broad bean, fennel, mint, lemon and Parmesan salad 100

fennel purée 66

sort-of-Waldorf salad 101

feta, mint, lentil and pistachio omelettes 20

figs: lamb shank and fig tagine 128

fishcakes, tuna Niçoise 103

five-spice soy roasted almonds 36

frittatas, smoked paprika chia 19

fritters: courgettes frites 44

quinoa and courgette fritters 40

fruit: tutti frutti clafoutis 155

G

gado gado Indonesian vegetable salad 87

garlic: red-eye aïoli 42

gas factor, pulses 11

gnocchi, baked white-bean 122

goats' curd: mushroom and goats' curd 'toasties' 16

savoury baked apples with goats' curd and Parma ham 70

granola parfaits, Black Forest 30

grapes: ajo blanco with red grapes 60

gratin, cauliflower and broccoli 73

green beans: green bean and tomato salad 92

'three beans' with basil pesto 75

green soup 62

guacamole 26

H

ham: choucroute 124

savoury baked apples with goats' curd and Parma ham 70

ultimate ham and lentil soup 50

hazelnuts: Brussels sprouts with hazelnuts, lentils and mustard dressing 72

chocolate hazelnut chews 148

orange, chocolate and hazelnut puddings 170

hummus: peppers stuffed with chia, hummus and pine nuts 98

I

Indonesian vegetable salad 87

J

jam: peanut butter and jam puddings 156

jamón: jamón salt 38

ultimate ham and lentil soup 50

jicama/yam beans: chicken san choi bow 96

K

kale: green soup 62
  kale caesar 84
  kale crisps with lemon 36
  white-bean colcannon 142
kelp/kombu 11
kidney beans 11
kimchee blankets, pigs in 39

L

lamb: lamb shank and fig tagine 128
  Moroccan lamb and chickpea burgers 111
latte custards 148
leeks: chickpeas, leek, apple and pear salad 75
lentils 10, 11
  Brussels sprouts with hazelnuts, lentils and mustard dressing 72
  dirty quinoa 114
  feta, mint, lentil and pistachio omelettes 20
  green soup 62
  lentil 'meatballs' 133
  tandoori salmon with spiced lentils and raita 108
  Turkish red lentil soup 51
  ultimate ham and lentil soup 50
lettuce: Moroccan lamb and chickpea burgers in lettuce leaves 111
  thyme-roasted chicken legs with braised baby lettuce and peas 134
linseed 10
lychees: chia, mango, coconut and macadamia trifle 155

M

mangos: chia, mango, coconut and macadamia trifle 155
meatballs: baked white-bean gnocchi with meatballs 122
  lentil 'meatballs' with ajvar and tomato 133
Mediterranean squid 112
meringue: Salzburger nockerl 158
Mexican baked eggs 26
milk: cinnamon coffee protein shakes 14
mint: mint-yoghurt dressing 111
  raita 108
miso aubergine 139
Moroccan lamb and chickpea burgers 111

mousse, peppermint chocolate with pistachios 168
muesli, chia Bircher 22
mung beans 11
mushrooms: mushroom and goats' curd 'toasties' 16
  pork, beef and mushroom-stuffed cabbage rolls 130
  quinoa-stuffed mushrooms 145
  sausages with leeks, caramelised onions, mushrooms and beans 138
  sticky braised beef 142

N

nougat: passionfruit and raspberry nougat parfait 161
nuts: Black Forest slow granola parfaits 30

O

oats: Black Forest slow granola parfaits 30
  chia Bircher muesli 22
omelettes: feta, mint, lentil and pistachio omelettes 20
onions: sausages with leeks, caramelised onions, mushrooms and beans 138
  smokey aubergine with tomatoes, pickled onion, parsley and pomegranate molasses 79
orange, chocolate and hazelnut puddings 170

P

padrón peppers with jamón salt 38
pancakes: almond blueberry pancakes 14
  socca with smoked salmon and whipped curds 28
panna cottas, yoghurt 152
papaya: Thai green papaya salad with trout 95
parfait, passionfruit and raspberry nougat 161
Parma ham, savoury baked apples with goats' curd and 70
passionfruit and raspberry nougat parfait 161
peaches: baked ricotta-stuffed peaches 162
  peach pulled pork with dirty quinoa 114
peanut butter: peanut butter and jam puddings 156
  spicy peanut sauce 87

pears: borlotti beans with roasted pear, walnuts and blue cheese 87
  cinnamon-poached pears 152
peas: green soup 62
  pea purée 67
  thyme-roasted chicken legs with braised baby lettuce and peas 134
  see also split peas
peppermint chocolate mousse 168
peppers: Mexican baked eggs 26
  padrón peppers with jamón salt 38
  peppers stuffed with chia, hummus and pine nuts 98
  piri piri chicken 116
Peruvian chicken and coriander soup 58
pesto: rocket, lemon and walnut pesto 53
  'three beans' with basil pesto 75
pigs in kimchee blankets 39
pine nuts, peppers stuffed with chia, hummus and 98
pinto beans 11
piri piri chicken 116
pistachio nuts: feta, mint, lentil and pistachio omelettes 20
  peppermint chocolate mousse with pistachios 168
pork: peach pulled pork with dirty quinoa 114
  pork, beef and mushroom-stuffed cabbage rolls 130
porridge, chia and apricot quinoa 23
prawns: prawn and quinoa grits 136
  prawn, avocado and edamame salad 106
prosciutto: gooey eggs with asparagus dippers 16
protein shakes, cinnamon coffee 14
pulses 10–11
purées 66–7

Q

quinoa 9
  chia and apricot quinoa porridge 23
  peach pulled pork with dirty quinoa 114
  pork, beef and mushroom-stuffed cabbage rolls 130
  prawn and quinoa grits 136
  quinoa aguadito (Peruvian chicken and coriander soup) 58
  quinoa and courgette fritters 40
  quinoa-stuffed mushrooms 145

R

radishes: duck breasts with roast beetroot, radish and cocoa 140
    radishes with butter and truffle salt 34
raita 108
raspberries: passionfruit and raspberry nougat parfait 161
    peanut butter and jam puddings 156
    raspberry, white bean and rose cake 164
rhubarb, apple and berry slow crumble 167
ribollita 53
rice malt syrup 10
ricotta: baked ricotta-stuffed peaches 162
    passionfruit and raspberry nougat parfait 161
rocket, lemon and walnut pesto 53

S

salads: broad bean, fennel, mint, lemon and Parmesan salad 100
    gado gado Indonesian vegetable salad 87
    green bean and tomato salad 92
    kale caesar 84
    prawn, avocado and edamame salad 106
    sort-of-Waldorf salad 101
    Thai green papaya salad with trout 95
salmon: tandoori salmon with spiced lentils and raita 108
salt, jamón 38
Salzburger nockerl 158
san choi bow, chicken 96
sauerkraut: choucroute 124
sausages: choucroute 124
    pigs in kimchee blankets 39
    sausages with leeks, caramelised onions, mushrooms and beans 138
    soft eggs with smokey baked beans 25
seabass swaddled in courgette ribbons 90
seaweed 11
smoked paprika chia frittatas 19
smoked salmon: socca with smoked salmon and whipped curds 28
socca with smoked salmon and whipped curds 28
sort-of-Waldorf salad 101
soufflés, blue cheese 120
soups: ajo blanco with red grapes 60
    all the nanas' chicken, lemon, egg and white bean soup 48
    chilled curried chickpea soup 57
    chilled white bean, cucumber, mint and yoghurt soup 56
    green soup 62
    quinoa aguadito (Peruvian chicken and coriander soup) 58
    ribollita 53
    roast Bloody Mary tomato soup 54
    Turkish red lentil soup 51
    ultimate ham and lentil soup 50
spices 11
split peas 11
    split pea purée 67
    yellow split peas with burnt butter and orange 80
squid: Mediterranean squid stuffed with white bean purée and olives 112
sweet potatoes: black bean, chorizo, sweet potato and coconut bowl 82

T

tagine, lamb shank and fig 128
tandoori salmon 108
tarka seasoning 78
tarta de Santiago, clementine 150
Thai green papaya salad with trout 95
'three beans' with basil pesto 75
thyme-roasted chicken legs 134
tofu: miso aubergine with ginger tofu and adzuki beans 139
tomatoes: aubergine 'parm' 127
    baked white-bean gnocchi with meatballs, mozzarella and tomato 122
    chilled curried chickpea soup 57
    green bean and tomato salad 92
    lentil 'meatballs' with ajvar and tomato 133
    Mediterranean squid 112
    Mexican baked eggs 26
    Moroccan lamb and chickpea burgers 111
    piri piri chicken with black beans and tomatoes 116
    pork, beef and mushroom-stuffed cabbage rolls 130
    roast Bloody Mary tomato soup 54
    roasted and fresh tomato skewers with mint and halloumi 40
    smoked paprika chia frittatas 19
    soft eggs with smokey baked beans 25
trifle: chia, mango, coconut and macadamia trifle 155
trout, Thai green papaya salad with 95
tuna: tuna Niçoise fishcakes 103
    vitello tonnato 92
Turkish red lentil soup 51
tutti frutti clafoutis 155

V

veal: vitello tonnato 92
vegetables: crudités 34
    ribollita 53
    see also peppers, tomatoes etc
vinegar, apple cider 10
vitello tonnato 92

W

walnuts: borlotti beans with roasted pear, walnuts and blue cheese 87
    rocket, lemon and walnut pesto 53
white beans: ajo blanco with red grapes 60
    all the nanas' chicken, lemon, egg and white bean soup 48
    baked white-bean gnocchi 122
    braised chicken with white beans, mustard and cider 144
    cannellini bean, Parmesan and artichoke dip 34
    chilled white bean, cucumber, mint and yoghurt soup 56
    Mediterranean squid stuffed with white bean purée and olives 112
    raspberry, white bean and rose cake 164
    ribollita 53
    roast Bloody Mary tomato soup 54
    sausages with leeks, caramelised onions, mushrooms and beans 138
    soft eggs with smokey baked beans 25
    'three beans' with basil pesto 75
    tuna Niçoise fishcakes 103
    white-bean colcannon 142
    white bean purée 67
white sauce 127

Y

yellow split peas with burnt butter and orange 80
yoghurt: chia Bircher muesli 22
    chilled white bean, cucumber, mint and yoghurt soup 56
    mint-yoghurt dressing 111
    raita 108
    yoghurt panna cottas 152

Acknowledgements

Thank you to all the luminous people who helped to make this book possible. It was a degree of serendipity which joined me once again with the remarkable Céline Hughes, without whose eagle eye, I'd be lost. To the rest of the kind folk at Quadrille, in particular Anne Furniss, Arielle Gamble and Helen Lewis, thank you for your stunning work. And thank you to Clare Hulton for your stewardship in finding this book such a happy home.

Eternal gratitude to Chris Chen for hosting a photoshoot that managed to be elegant, efficient and welcoming to the whims of an 11-week-old baby boy, and to Kirsty and Nick for making it all come together so smoothly.

My love goes to the friends who helped test recipes, in particular Tristan, Sharon, May, Alice, Melissa M and Ted, and to the others who so kindly chipped in with 'Willwatch' while I cooked and scrawled notes in a notebook.

Lastly, to my family: thank you for helping me believe that anything is possible, and for your support in making it so.

Editorial director Anne Furniss
Creative director Helen Lewis
Senior editor Céline Hughes
Designer Arielle Gamble
Production James Finan and Vincent Smith
Food & prop stylist Kirsty Cassidy
Home economist Nick Banbury

First published in 2014 by
Quadrille Publishing Limited
www.quadrille.co.uk

Text © 2014 Tori Haschka
Photography © 2014 Chris Chen
Design and layout © 2014 Quadrille Publishing Limited

The rights of the author have been asserted.

ISBN 978 1 84949 465 6

Printed in China

The publisher would like to thank the following ceramicists for their kind loan of props for the photoshoots:

David Edmonds, www.davidedmonds.com.au

Chinaclay, www.chinaclay.com.au

The FortyNine Studio, www.thefortynine.com.au

Sian Thomas, www.sianthomas.net

Joanna Gambatto, Sweet Potato Ceramics,
  www.sweetpotato.net.au

Yew Kong Tham, www.ginkgoleaf.com.au

A note on the recipes

Timings are guidelines for conventional ovens. If you are using a fan-assisted oven, set your oven temperature to approximately 15°C lower. Use an oven thermometer to check the temperature.